DARK HORIZON

おとなになったら使うかも知れない
基礎英語

SEASON 1

ブライアン・レイス著

INTRODUCTION

はじめに

　幸か不幸か!? 私は『New Horizon』を使って英語を教えていた経験があります。テキストを使った授業は、先生次第で楽しくも退屈にもなったりします。当時教師だった私は、テキストのまま使うのではなく、楽しく学べるように工夫したのが、この本が生まれるきっかけになりました。

　そこで英語を楽しく学んでくれる方法のひとつに、登場人物の声を変えて、バックストーリーを加えてみました。それぞれのキャラクターを異なった声で、思いついた厄介なシナリオで生徒に読み聞かせていったのです。そうするとそれぞれのキャラクターがイキイキと活きて、生徒は私が作り上げたストーリーを純粋に楽しんでくれたようでした。彼らは、想像上のストーリーで、マイク、エミ、慎がどのように問題解決をしていったらよいのか、一緒に考えて英語のみならず想像力を養ってくれたのではないかと思っています。そんないきさつから、この本のアイディアが生まれました。

　中学時代から10年経ち、あの大好きだったキャラクターたちが年を取り、さらに賢くなって中学校では学べなかった大人の英語を教えに帰ってくるストーリーを考えました。あくまでも勝手に妄想したジョークたっぷりの物語ですが、大人になって現実の社会で使えるかもしれない!? 英語のフレーズが沢山入っています。当時、彼らにそんな英語フレーズを教えていたら大問題になっていたかも知れませんが、今ならきっと大丈夫だと確信しています。現在大学で学んでいたり、就職している私の教え子たちが当時の授業のことを思い出しながら、また英語を勉強中のサラリーマンや社会人にちょっとした息抜きに笑いながら読んでいただけたら幸いです。内容には細心の注意を払っておりますが、一部の皆様にご不安やご不快な思いをさせてしまう可能性があります。またご使用された際に第三者を傷つけたり、損害の責任が発生した際には責任を負えませんことを予めご了承ください。最後になりますが、両親を始め、ミカ、アヤ、ジミ、アダム、ユーコ、アナスタシア、ポール、ジェームス、オブキタ、アカシナ、ジャスティン、ゴードン、ジェイソンにお礼を言いたいです。ありがとうございました。

ブライアン

I was lucky or unlucky enough to have taught English in Japan using the New Horizon textbook. Textbook lessons can be as fun or dull as teacher makes them. I found the textbook to be boring and wholly uninteresting, but it was up to me to make the lessons fun. One way I did that was by giving the characters in the book their own voices and back story.

I often made silly references to pop culture, read the stories in different voices and came up with troublesome scenarios for the characters. I think my students at the time genuinely enjoyed the stories. They often had input on how Mike, Emi or Shin might go about solving their issues. This book grew out of those stories.

I hope my former students who are now in university or starting their new jobs will remember our classes together. There are also plenty of useful real world English phrases in this book. I would have gotten in trouble if I had taught them then, but I can teach you now.

Now 10 years later, older and wiser, your favorite characters are back to teach you what you didn't learn in junior high.

Brian

Thank You For Your Help And Support,
Mika, Aya, Jimi, Adam, Yuko, Anastasia, Paul, James,
Obukita, Akashina, Justin, Gordon, Jason, and Mom & Dad

CONTENTS 目次

はじめに	002
登場人物紹介	006
登場人物関係図	011
Chapter 1　マイク・デイビス　Mike Davis	035
Chapter 2　アン・グリーン　Ann Green	047
Chapter 3　伊藤 エミ　Emi Ito	059
Chapter 4　ジュディ・ブラウン　Judy Brown	073

Chapter 5 石川 コージ　Koji Ishikawa ……………………………………………… 085

Chapter 6 リサ・グリーン　Lisa Green …………………………………………… 097

Chapter 7 田中 慎　Shin Tanaka ………………………………………………… 109

Chapter 8 佐藤 カズコ　Kazuko Sato ……………………………………………… 121

Chapter 9 ビリー・グリーン　Billie Green ………………………………………… 133

Chapter 10 ビン・ドン　Bin Dong ………………………………………………… 145

インデックス ……………………………………………………………………… 157

CHARACTER INTRODUCTION
登場人物紹介

本書に出てくる愛すべきキャラクターをご紹介。

Most used phrase:
よく使うフレーズ:

> Fuck my life.
> 人生くそくらえ

Mike Davis
マイク・デイビス

Age: 25歳　ホームレス

--

Frequents: Yoyogi Park
Hobbies: Smoking, drinking, talking about idols with Koji
Favorite Food: Cup Noodle curry flavor
Favorite Drink: Anything with alcohol

出没場所: 代々木公園
趣味: たばこ、お酒、コージとアイドル話をすること
好きな食べ物: カップヌードルカレー味
好きな飲み物: アルコールならなんでも

Ann Green
アン・グリーン

Age: 38歳　クラブオーナー兼ママ

--

Frequents: Ginza
Hobbies: Singing Enka, Mixing sleeping pills and alcohol.
Favorite Food: Zaru Soba Noodles
Favorite Drink: Vodka on the rocks

出没場所: 銀座
趣味: 演歌を歌う、睡眠薬とアルコールを一緒に飲むこと
好きな食べ物: ざる蕎麦
好きな飲み物: ウォッカロック

Most used phrase:
よく使うフレーズ:

> I just want to make the pain stop.
> この痛みを止めたいだけなのよ

Emi Ito

伊藤エミ

Age: 24歳　ホステス、売春婦

--

Frequents: Kabukicho and Ikebukuro West Side
Hobbies: Purikura, Shopping, Drugs
Favorite Food: Kyushu Style Tonkotsu Ramen
Favorite Drink: Cosmopolitan

出没場所: 歌舞伎町、池袋ウエストサイド
趣味: プリクラ、ショッピング、麻薬
好きな食べ物: 九州とんこつラーメン
好きな飲み物: コスモポリタン
　　　　　　　（ウォッカベースのカクテル）

Most used phrase:
よく使うフレーズ:

> I don't do anything for free.
> お金くれるなら
> なんでもやるわ

Most used phrase:
よく使うフレーズ:

> Talk to the hand!
> もういいわ

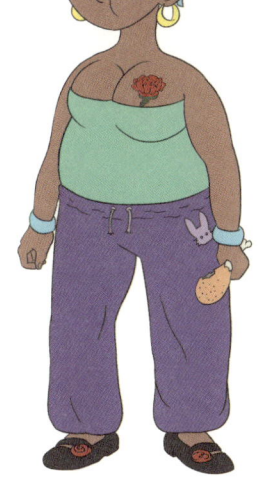

Judy Brown

ジュディ・ブラウン

Age: 25歳　ホステス、バリスタ

--

Frequents: Naka-Meguro
Hobbies: Eating Gourmet, Karaoke
Favorite Food: Hamburger
Favorite Drink: Beer

出没場所: 渋谷
趣味: グルメ料理を食べる、カラオケ
好きな食べ物: ハンバーガー
好きな飲み物: ビール

CHARACTER INTRODUCTION

Most used phrase:
よく使うフレーズ:

> You're such a n00b!
> お前って初心者だな！

10年前

Koji Ishikawa
石川コージ

Age: 45歳　無職、アイドルオタク

--

Frequents: Akihabara
Hobbies: Collecting panties, AV, idol concerts
Favorite Food: Rice Omelets
Favorite Drink: Kahlua Milk

出没場所: 秋葉原
趣味: 女性もの下着集め、AV、アイドルコンサート
好きな食べ物: オムライス
好きな飲み物: カルーアミルク

Most used phrase:
よく使うフレーズ:

> You call yourself a man !?
> それでも男!?

10年前

Lisa Green
リサ・グリーン

Age: 39歳　バイクの修理工、レズビアン

--

Frequents: Yokohama, Akasaka
Hobbies: Formula 1, Fixing Bikes, Basketball
Favorite Food: Waffles with maple syrup
Favorite Drink: Whiskey Coke

出没場所: 横浜、赤坂
趣味: F1、バイク修理、バスケットボール
好きな食べ物: メープルシロップをたっぷりかけたワッフル
好きな飲み物: ウィスキーコーク

Most used phrase:
よく使うフレーズ:

> Get outta my face, I'll mess you up!
> 消えろ、さもないとボッコボコにするぞ

Shin Tanaka
田中慎

Age: 25歳　ヤンキー

--

Frequents: Odaiba
Hobbies: Riding motorcyles, hostess clubs
Favorite Food: Shoyu Ramen with chilli pepper
Favorite Drink: Ramune

出没場所: お台場
趣味: バイク、ホステス（エミ）がいるクラブ通い
好きな食べ物: 唐辛子をたっぷりかけた醤油ラーメン
好きな飲み物: ラムネ

10年前

Most used phrase:
よく使うフレーズ:

> You are no match for me!
> わたしにはかなわないね

10年前

Kazuko Sato
佐藤カズコ

Age: 39歳　元教師、元女子プロレスラー、
　　　　カフェオーナー、レズビアン

--

Frequents: Ryogoku
Hobbies: Wrestling, Sumo, Karate, Judo
Favorite Food: Miso-Katsu
Favorite Drink: Shochu

出没場所: 両国
趣味: レスリング、相撲、空手、柔道
好きな食べ物: 味噌カツ
好きな飲み物: 焼酎

CHARACTER INTRODUCTION

Most used phrase:
よく使うフレーズ:

Fabulous! すてき!

🇨🇦

Billie(Bill) Green
ビリー・グリーン

Age: 23歳　フィットネスクラブオーナー兼トレーナー、
　　　　女装好き、アンとリサ・グリーンの弟

--

Frequents: Harajuku, Shinjuku 2-chome
Hobbies: Yoga, Shopping, Fashion
Favorite Food: Pancakes
Favorite Drink: Jello Shots

出没場所: 原宿、新宿2丁目
趣味: ヨガ、ショッピング、オシャレ
好きな食べ物: パンケーキ
好きな飲み物: ジェローショット(ウォッカが入ったゼリー)

Most used phrase:
よく使うフレーズ:

What the fuck you looking at punk?
なに見てんだよ?

🇨🇳

Bing Dong
ビン・ドン

Age: 43歳　三合会メンバー(マフィア)

--

Frequents: Kabukicho, China Town
Hobbies: Mahjong Parlors, Soap Lands, Darts,
　　　　　　Throwing Knives, Air BB guns.
Favorite Food: Dumplings, Peking duck
Favorite Drink: Dom Perignon

出没場所: 歌舞伎町、中華街
趣味: 雀荘、ソープランド、ダーツ、ナイフ投げ、エアBBガン
好きな食べ物: 餃子、北京ダック
好きな飲み物: ドンペリ

DARK HORIZON関係図

中学校を出たあと、みんないろいろなことがありました。
関係図を見てみましょう。

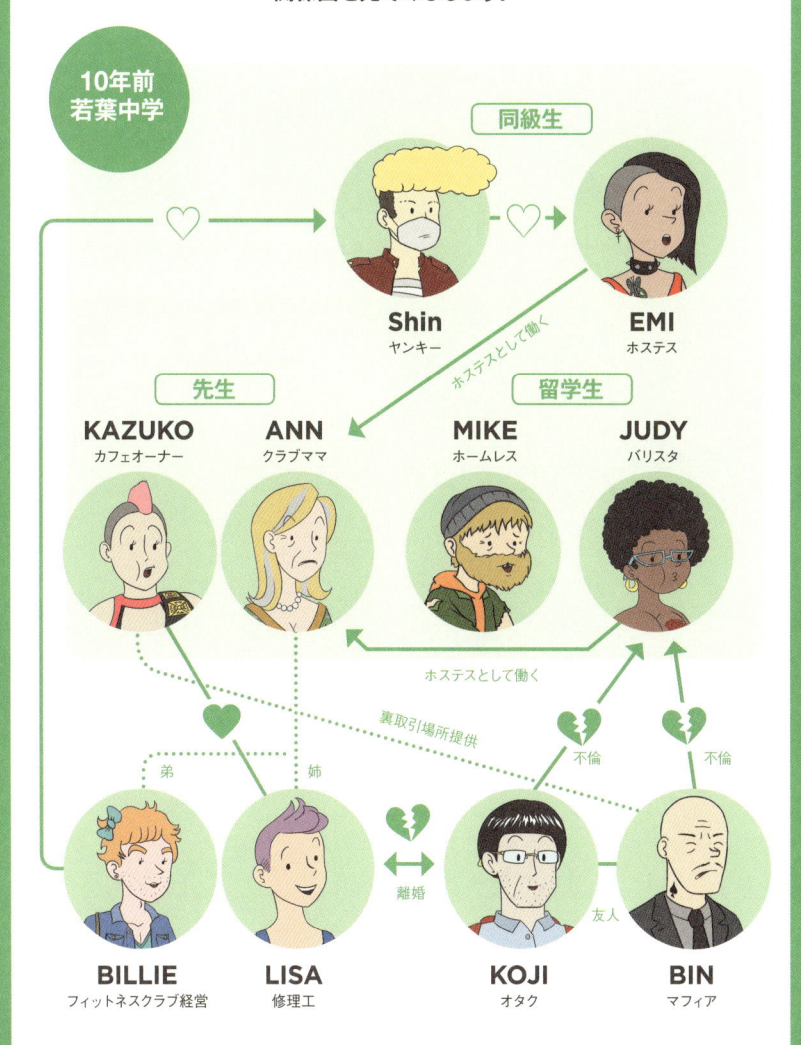

10年前 若葉中学

同級生

Shin ヤンキー ♡→ **EMI** ホステス

先生: **KAZUKO** カフェオーナー / **ANN** クラブママ

留学生: **MIKE** ホームレス / **JUDY** バリスタ

Shin → ホステスとして働く

BILLIE フィットネスクラブ経営 — 弟
LISA 修理工 — 姉
KOJI オタク
BIN マフィア

LISA ↔ KOJI 離婚
KOJI — BIN 友人
KOJI → JUDY 不倫 💔
BIN → JUDY 不倫 💔
ANN → JUDY ホステスとして働く
KAZUKO — 裏取引場所提供
BILLIE ♡ (KAZUKO方面)

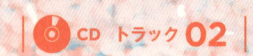

Mike's Life Scenario 1
マイクの人生シナリオ1「花見タイム」

マイクが帰宅したときの会話。

1: Spare some change?

3: How about some booze?

5: No! Get off my porch!

2: Fuck off old man!

4: Go away, you stink!

6: Oh sorry!

1: Hit me with a double this time.

3: Don't tell me what to do bitch!

5: I'm sorry Ann, it's just, I found out I'm impotent.

7: Thanks.

Ann's Life Scenario 2
アンの人生シナリオ2「クラブ若葉で」

コージがアンの経営するホステスクラブに来店した。

2: I think you've had enough Koji.
4: What the fuck Koji, what is your problem?
6: Oh my! So you can only shoot blanks? Ok, next one's on the house.

Emi's Life Scenario 3
エミの人生シナリオ3「ラブホテルにて」
慎はエミをホテルに呼んだ。

1: Oh yeah baby, who is your daddy?

3: What do you mean? Can't you tell I'm hitting your ovaries!

2: Huh? Did you start yet?
4: Did you stick it in already? I can't feel anything.

Judy's Life Scenario 4
ジュディの人生シナリオ4「コーヒーショップ」

ジュディは客のビリーに対して横柄な態度をとる。

1: I said no whip on my coffee three times, you dumb bitch.

3: Skank!

5: I have never been so insulted!

PISS........ ¥20
CREAM.... ¥1980
WATER..... ¥680
2: Who are you calling a bitch, bitch!
JUDITH
4: Talk to the hand!
SEA BITCH COFFEE

Koji's Life Scenario 5
コージの人生シナリオ5「アイドルコンサートにて」

コージとマイクは人気アイドルコンサートへ行った。

1: Oh my god they are so cute!

3: There is no way you will get past security. But I can do one better.

5: I have some exclusive upskirts of the girls, only 500 yen a piece.

2: Do you think I can get backstage? I want to see them up close.
4: What?
6: That's like 30 beer cans per picture man! Too rich for me!

Lisa's Life Scenario 6
リサの人生シナリオ6「バイク修理屋」

テクニシャンのリサが慎にアドバイスする。

2: HAHAHA!

4: You need to be creative Shin. Use your hands, oral sex, or in your case maybe a strap-on.

6: Hell no!

1: Can you give me some advice? Emi said my dick was small.

3: Don't laugh, this is serious! You don't have any dick at all, how do you even have sex?

5: Strap-ons! Can I borrow one of yours?

CD トラック **26**

1: Get back here, you little shit!

3: When I catch you, you're dead Shin! You hear me, punk?

Shin's Life Scenario 7
慎の人生シナリオ7「ハイウェイにて」
慎はエリミネーターから逃げる。

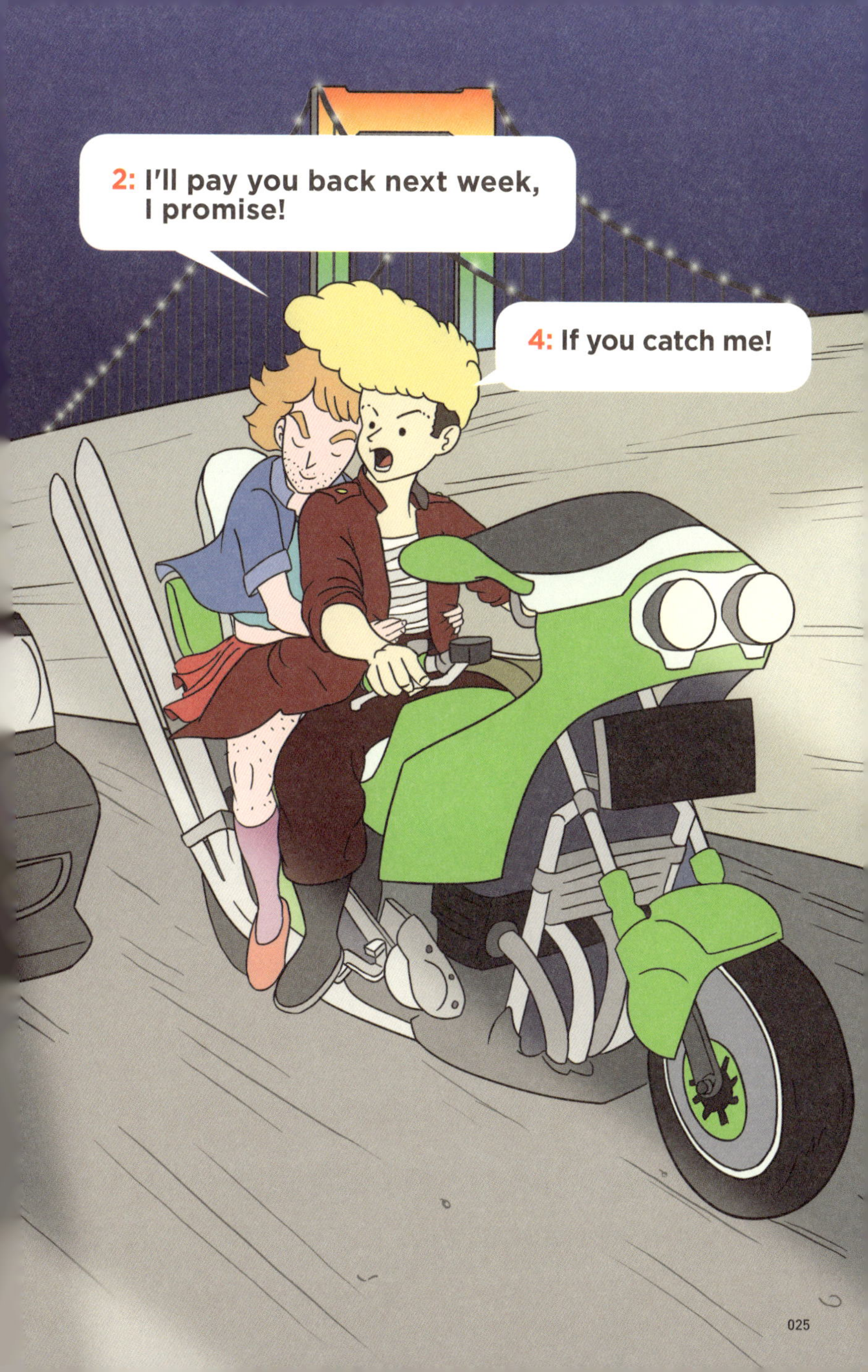
2: I'll pay you back next week, I promise!
4: If you catch me!

Kazuko's Life Scenario 8
カズコの人生シナリオ8「相撲観戦」
カズコは生まれて初めて相撲を見に行った。

1: Yeah! Destroy him! Body slam! Headlock!

3: What? No flying clothesline? Pile Driver? Jump kick to the face?

5: Ohhh...

2: I don't think they are allowed to do that in this sport.

4: No, No and No. This is traditional Japanese wrestling!

CD トラック **34**

2: **It's important to open your chakras for optimal flow of energy.**

4: **Nonsense, it's good for your spiritual energy!**

6: **No pain, no gain. Now spread 'em!**

Billie's Life Scenario 9
ビリーの人生シナリオ9「フィットネススタジオ」

ビリーは一生懸命ヨガのポーズを教える。

1: I don't know if I feel comfortable doing that pose.
3: Yes, but I feel exposed.
5: It looks painful!

Bin's Life Scenario 10
ビンの人生シナリオ10「雀荘にて」
ギャンブルをするマイクは大ピンチに陥る。

1: You cheater!

3: Are you calling me a liar?

5: Watch what you say! You might be gambling with more than some chips, you could be gambling with your life.

2: Bullshit! You're cheating!

4: That's right! You're nothing but a two-bit criminal!

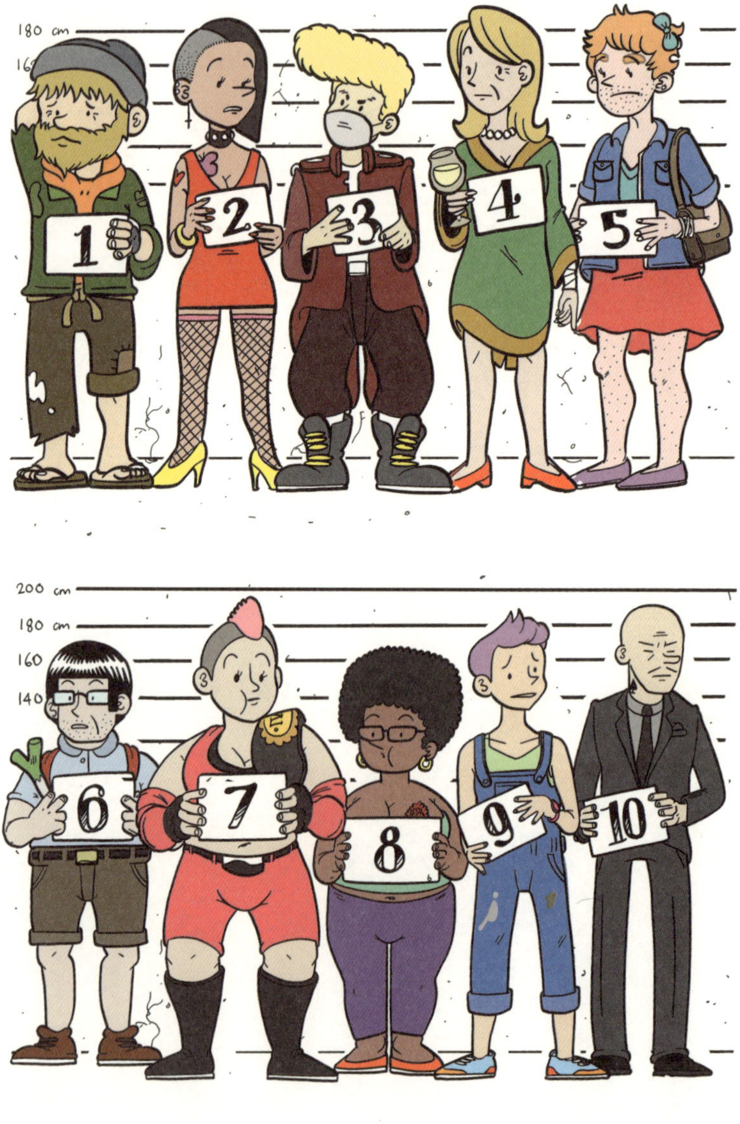
180 cm
1
2
3
4
5
200 cm
180 cm
160
140
6
7
8
9
10

HOW TO USE

本書の使い方と注意点

誠に勝手ながら、登場人物の10年後を想定して作った物語形式の英語学習書です。あくまでも妄想したストーリーということを念頭に置きながら、自身の人生にもしものことがあっても大丈夫なように備えてしっかりと習得しておきましょう。

◎長文読解

まずは、チャプター1～10まで10人の登場人物の10年後の人生物語を読んで理解しましょう。次にリスニングCDでネイティブが話す英語を何度も聞き、なにを語っているか聞き取れるようにしましょう。これをすらすら言えるようになったら、あなたの英語もネイティブに近づけるでしょう。

◎英単語を使った例短文

人生物語で使われた単語を使って、英短文を作ってみましょう。慣れたら自分なりの例文を作って、恥ずかしがらずに日常生活で使ってみるのが上達のコツです。

◎会話形式シナリオ

それぞれキャラクター人生のワンシーンを切り取った会話です。まずは読んで理解し、リスニングCDでネイティブの英会話を聞いてみましょう。実際に自分なりにキャラクター別に声色を変えてしゃべってみましょう。スムーズに言えるまで何回かCDを聞いて、日常でも試してみましょう。

◎英語フレーズ

キャラクターの職業(!?)に合わせたフレーズのやりとりを用意しました。かなり極端な人生を送っているので、もしかしたら使わないかも知れませんが、これがアメリカンジョークということを理解できるでしょう。もちろん、使えるフレーズはどんどん使いこなしてみましょう。日本語と英語で入っているので、睡眠しながら聞けば習得はもちろん、ネイティブになる夢を見るかもしれません。

HOW TO USE

◎GOODとBADフレーズ

会話形式のシナリオにある重要な単語を使って、言っても良いのと悪い文を掲載しています。自身の性格に合っているのならば、バッドな文を中心に覚えていきましょう。こちらも声を出してみるのが効率よく覚える近道となります。

◎ローマ字表記

日本の方ならば、漢字の読みは問題ないと思いますが、ネイティブや外国人のお友達に日本語ではどう言うのかを教える場合を考えてローマ字を入れています。お互いのジョークの理解度や違い、また文化を共有するためには、最適なプレゼントとなることでしょう。

◎リスニングCD

英語は、耳から入るのが一番の近道とも言えます。このリスニングCDを聞けば、「総合力」と「応用力」がつく英語力を養えるはずです。物語に合ったBGMも入っているので、ちょっとしたラジオドラマを聞く感覚で楽しく聞けるようになっています。家の掃除をしながら、洗い物をしながら、寝る前など音楽を聞くように普段の生活にも流すと自然とネイティブ英語が身につくかもしれません。

内容には細心の注意を払っておりますが、一部の皆様にご不安やご不快な思いをさせてしまう可能性があります。またご使用された際に第三者を傷つけたり、損害の責任が発生した際には責任を負えませんことを予めご了承ください。この英語を実践的なのかは各自でご判断いただき、扱いには注意して使いましょう。

CHAPTER 1

MIKE DAVIS
マイク・デイビス

Mike Davis's Life Story
マイク・デイビスの人生

中学生だったマイクも25歳になりました。
どんな人生を送っているのか見てみましょう。

Mike's Life Story

After a brief career looking for a big break as a foreign talent on Japanese TV, Mike eventually found himself out of money. He tried teaching at various English language schools but was fired again and again for sexual harassment of his students. No stranger to anger management issues, he is still bitter about his messy breakup with Emi Itou. Now with no money and his visa status in question, Mike collects cans to help fuel his alcohol addiction.

日本のテレビ界で外タレとして大ブレークを狙い続けたあと、やがてマイクは金欠に陥ったことを知った。あちこちの英語学校で先生としてやってみたが、生徒へのセクハラが原因でいつもクビ。カッとする怒りをうまく処理できるようなよそ者などいるわけもなく、彼はまだ伊藤エミとの泥沼な別れを引きずっていた。今は金もなければ、滞在ビザもやばい。マイクは缶を拾い集めて、自分のアル中を満足させる足しにしていた。

Nihon no terebi-kai de gaitare toshite daiburēku wo nerai tsudzuketa ato, yagate maiku wa kinketsu ni ochītta koto wo shitta. Achikochi no eigo gakkō de sensei to shite yatte mitaga, seito e no sekuhara ga gen'in de, itsumo kubi. Katto suru ikari wo umaku shori dekiru yōna yosomono nado iru wake mo naku, kare wa mada Itō Emi to no doronumana wakare wo hikizutte ita. Ima wa kane monakereba, taizai biza mo yabai. Maiku wa kan wo hiroi atsumete, jibun no aruchū wo manzoku sa seru tashi ni shite ita.

Spring season in Japan is when I like to get drunk off of leftover booze from hanami parties. I also make a lot of money collecting cans in the park! Hanami is my favorite time of the year!

春になると花見で飲み残したお酒を拾って、そのお酒で酔っ払うのが好き。そして公園で拾った缶も集めるとたくさんお金がもらえるんだ。だから花見の時期が一番好き！

Haru ni naru to hanami de nomi nokoshita osake wo hirotte, sono osake de yopparau no ga suki. Soshite kouen de hirotta kan mo atsumeru to takusan okane ga moraerun da. Dakara hanami no jiki ga ichiban suki!

CHAPTER **1** Words from the story used in phrases

Words from the story used in phrases

物語の単語を使って例文を作る

マイクの人生ストーリーのキーワードを使って例文を作ってみましょう。

Words from the story　ストーリーのキーワード

Big Break
大ブレーク

Fired
首になる

Sexual Harassment
セクハラ

Addiction
中毒

Key Word_01

Big Break 大ブレーク

Dai burēku

All those blonde bimbos in Los Angeles are hoping to get their big break in Hollywood.

LAにいる金髪バカ女たちはハリウッドで芸能人になって大ブレークすると思っている。

LA ni iru kinpatsu bakaonna-tachi wa Hariuddo de geinōjin ni natte dai burēku suru to omotte iru.

Key Word_02
Fired 首になる
Kubi ni naru

He was fired for pulling his cock out in front of the boss's wife.

彼は社長の奥さんの前でチ●コを出したので首になった。

Kare wa shachō no okusan no mae de chi●ko wo dashita node kubi ni natta.

Key Word_03
Sexual Harassment セクハラ
Sekuhara

She will file for sexual harassment if she catches you taking pictures up her skirt.

彼女のスカートの中を盗撮したことがバレたら、セクハラで訴えられるよ。

kanojo no sukato no naka wo tousatsu shita koto ga baretara, sekuhara de utaerareru yo.

Key Word_04
Addiction 中毒
Chudoku

Drinking too much alcohol can become an addiction, but if you enjoy it, maybe it can be your hobby.

飲みすぎるとアル中になるけど、楽しくお酒を飲むことは、趣味のようなものだ。

Nomi sugiruto aruchū ni narukedo, tanoshiku osake wo nomu koto wa, shumi no yōna monoda.

CHAPTER 1 Mike's Life Scenario 1 | CD トラック 02

Mike's Life Scenario 1
マイクの人生シナリオ1「花見タイム」

マイクが帰宅したときの会話。

1: Spare some change?
お金をくれません?
Okane wo kuremasen?

3: How about some booze?
じゃあ酒くれよ。
Jyaa sake kureyo.

5: No! Get off my porch!
ふざげるな！お前らが
オレのベランダからうせろ！
Fusageruna! Omaera ga ore no beranda kara usero!

2: Fuck off old man!
どっか行けよジジイ!
Dokka ikeyo jiji!

4: Go away, you stink!
うせろ!マジくせー!
Usero! Maji kuse!

6: Oh sorry!
あっ、悪い。
A, warui.

Important Phrases 重要なフレーズ

※ **Spare some change** (スペア サム チェンジ)
お金を欲しいと優しく言う言い方。 A polite way of asking for money.

※ **Fuck off** (ファックオフ)
誰かを追い払うときに使う無礼な言い方。 A rude way of telling people to leave you alone.

※ **Booze** (ブーズ)
アルコールの俗語。 A slang term for alcohol

Mike -what a homeless person would say...
ホームレスのマイクが使うフレーズ11

使うのに注意=☠　注意=☠☠　かなり危険=☠☠☠

Phrase_01
I am too poor to eat.

貧しすぎて食べれないんだよ。

Mazushisugite taberarenaindayo

Phrase_02
That's not just any stack of boxes, that's my house!

それはただのダンボールの山じゃなくてオレの家なんだよ！

Sore wa tada no danboru no yama jyanakute ore no ie nan dayo!

Phrase_03
Japan is the best place to be homeless!

日本はホームレスにとって最高の場所なんだよ！

Nihon wa homresu ni totte saikou no basho nan dayo!

Phrase_04
Can I have those cans when you are finished?

その缶、終わったらオレにくれない？

Sono kan owattara ore ni kurenai?

Phrase_05
I'm not homeless, I'm free!

オレはホームレスじゃなくて自由人だ！

Ore wa homresu jyanakute jiyujin da!

Phrase_06 ☠
I will work for food/sex/money/drugs/alcohol!
食べ物、セックス、金、ヤク、酒のためだったらなんでもやるぜ！

tabemono, sekkusu, kane, yaku, sake no tamedattara nan demo yaruze!

Phrase_07
When you're homeless, everyday is a holiday!
ホームレスになると、毎日が休日だぜ！

Homuresu ni naruto mainichi ga kyujitsu daze!

Phrase_08
Everything the light touches※ is my home.
ここすべての場所がオレのもんだ！

Koko subete no basho ga ore no mono da!

Phrase_09
※One man's trash is another man's treasure!
捨てる神あれば拾う神あり。

Suteru kami areba hirou kami ari.

Phrase_10
I may be drunk, but you are ugly, and tomorrow I will be ※sober.
今酔っ払ってるが、明日には酔いがさめる。でもお前は一生ブス！

Ima yotteru ga ashita ni wa yoi ga sameru, demo omae wa issho busu!

Phrase_11
I did not chose this life, it chose me.
オレがこの人生を選んだんじゃない、人生がオレを選んだんだ！

Ore ga kono jinsei wo erandan janai, jinsei ga ore wo erandanda!

※Phrase_08: light touchesは、ライオンキングにある台詞「太陽が届くところはすべて我らの王国だ」からのフレーズを引用したもの。

※Phrase_09: 英訳すると「ある人によってのゴミは別の人にとっては宝」という、この世の中はいろいろなことがある意味の英語のことわざです。

※Phrase_10: soberは酔いがさめた、しらふのこと。酔っていないときに使うのがポイント。

Mike -What to say to homeless...
ホームレスのマイクに使うフレーズ10

> 使うのに注意=☠ 注意=☠☠ かなり危険=☠☠☠

Phrase_01
Your house is so dirty you have to wipe your feet to go outside.
お前の家クソ汚いから外に行くのに足ふかなきゃいけないな！
Omae no ie kuso kitanai kara soto ni iku no ni ashi fukanakya ikenain na!

Phrase_02
Soap is not your enemy.
石鹸はお前の敵じゃねーよ。
Sekken wa omae no tekijyane yo.

Phrase_03 ☠
Get a job you worthless sack of shit!
仕事見つけろよ、このクソ野郎！
Shigoto mitsukero yo, kono kusoyaro!

Phrase_04
Don't come any closer!
これ以上、近づくんじゃねーよ！
Kore ijo chikatzukun jyane yo!

Phrase_05 ☠
You reek like shit!
お前ウンコくせー！
Omae unko kuse!

Phrase_06
What a lovely blue tarp home※ you have.
ブルーシートでできた家がとても素敵ですね!

Burushito de dekita ie ga totemo suteki desu ne!

Phrase_07
If I gave you any cash, then I'd be poor.
お前に金をやったら、オレが貧乏になっちゃうよ!

Omae ni kane wo yattara, ore ga binbo ni nacchau yo!

Phrase_08 ☠☠
It looks like someone shit in your mouth※.
誰かがウンコしたみたいな口してるな。

Dare ka ga unko shita mitai na kuchi shiteru na.

Phrase_09
Here's a 10 yen coin, don't spend it all in one place※.
ほら、10円玉やるから、賢く使えよ。

Hora 10en dama, kashikoku tsukae yo.

Phrase_10
If I give you money, will you go away?
もし金をやったら、失せてくれるか?

Moshi kane wo yattara usetekureru ka?

※Phrase_03:sack of shitは、直訳するとうんこの入った袋のこと。価値のないことを意味し、人を非難するときにも使われる。

※Phrase_06:海外では、基本は段ボールしか使われませんが、blue tarp homeは、日本独特のものと言えるでしょう。

※Phrase_08:ウンコしたみたいな口は、口臭がきつく、黄ばんだ歯の人に対して使う失礼な言い方。

※Phrase_09:all in one placeは、ひとつの場所やものを使い切らないでということ。お酒やギャンブルで使い切る場合などに使う。

CHAPTER 1 Helpful Words And Phrases GOOD & BAD

シナリオに関連する単語を使ったGOODとBADフレーズ

Helpful Words And Phrases
GOOD & BAD

Spring 春 Haru

GOOD
Spring is my favorite season of the year.
春は一年でいちばん好きな季節です。
Haru wa ichinen de ichiban suki na kisetsu desu.

BAD
Spring is my favorite season because that's when all the bitches wear short skirts.
春ってのはオレの一番好きな季節だ。なぜって、女どもが皆ミニスカートをはくからな。
Haru tte no wa ore no ichiban sukina kisetsuda. Naze tte, onna-domo ga minna minisukato wo hakukara na.

Picnic ピクニック Pikunikku

GOOD
The girl brought sandwiches to the picnic for her friends.
ピクニックに女の子は友達のためにサンドイッチを持ってきた。
Pikunikku ni on'nanoko wa tomodachi no tame ni sandoitchi wo motte kita.

BAD
Fuck your picnic and fuck your sandwiches, give me some weed!
ピクニックがなんだってんだ、サンドイッチがなんだってんだ、マリファナよこせよ!
Pikuniku ga nandattenn da, sandoicchi ga nan dattenda, marifana yokose yo.

Trash ゴミ Gomi

GOOD
Please separate your trash into burnable and non-burnable bins.
ゴミは燃えるゴミと燃えないゴミに分別してください。
Gomi wa moeru gomi to moenai gomi ni bunbetsu shite kudasai.

BAD
Just leave everything there, who gives a shit about the Earth!
そこらへんに置いとけよ、誰が地球環境なんて気にすんだよ!
Sokorahen ni oiteoke yo, dare ga chikyoukankyou nante ki ni sun dayo!

Cherry Blossom 桜 Sakura

GOOD
Cherry blossoms only bloom for a short time each year.
桜は毎年短い期間にのみ咲く。
Sakura wa maitoshi mijikai kikan ninomi saku.

BAD
Cherry blossoms are fucking beautiful.
桜ってのはすっげーきれいだぜ!
Sakura tteno wa sugge kirei da ze!

CHAPTER 2

ANN GREEN
アン・グリーン

Ann Green's Life Story
アン・グリーンの人生

カナダから来た英語の先生もいろいろありました。
どんな人生を送っているのか見てみましょう。

Ann's Life Story

Unhappy only teaching English in Japan, she began moonlighting as a hostess, where her blonde hair and good looks earned her 10x her teaching wages. Things were not always easy though and she fell into a deep depression, attempting suicide on multiple occasions. After being released from a mental hospital a few months back, she got in contact with her former students Emi and Judy. After successfully blackmailing her former students into working for her, she started her own hostess club.

日本で英語を教えるだけではつまらなくて、彼女はホステスとして副業を始めた。そこでは彼女の金髪やルックスのおかげで、英語教師として働くよりも10倍多く稼げた。だが、ことはそううまくはいかない。重いうつ病となり、何度も自殺を試みるようになる。精神病院に数ヶ月入院し、ようやく退院してかつての教え子のエミとジュディに連絡を取った。彼女らを脅かすことに成功すると、自らホステスクラブを始めて働かせたのだった。

Nihon de eigo wo oshieru dakede wa tsumaranakute, kanojo wa hosutesu toshite fukugyō wo hajimeta. Sokode wa kanojo no kinpatsu ya rukkusu no okage de, eigo kyōshi to shite hataraku yori mo 10-bai ōku kasegeta. Daga, koto wa sō umaku wa ikanai. Omoi utsubyō to nari, nando mo jisatsu wo kokoromiru yō ni naru. Seishinbyōin ni sū-kagetsu nyūin shi, yōyaku taiin shite katsute no oshiego no Emi to Judi ni renraku wo totta. Kanojora wo odokasu koto ni seikō suru to, mizukara hosutesukurabu wo hajimete hatarakaseta no datta.

My hostess club is really just a gathering of people with shattered dreams. Tired salarymen, drugs, alcohol, and broken girls. I should just end it all right now... but not before my girls squeeze every last penny out of these customers.

私のホステスクラブは夢が叶わなかった人たちが集ってくるところなのよ。(人生に男にお金に)捨てられた女たちとアルコール、ドラッグ、疲れきったサラリーマンまでいる。もうすべてを終わりにしたほうがいいかもね……　でももちろんこの子たちが客の金をすべてしぼりとってからね。

Watashi no hosustesu kurabu wa yume ga kanawanakatta hitotachi ga atsumete kuru tokoro nano yo. (Jinsei ni otoko ni okane ni) suterareta on'natachi to arukōru, doraggu, tsukare kitta sararīman made iru. Mou subete wo owari ni shita hō ga ī kamo ne……. Demo mochiron kono ko-tachi ga kyaku no kane wo subete shibori tottekara ne.

CHAPTER 2 Words from the story used in phrases

Words from the story used in phrases

物語の単語を使って例文を作る

アンの人生ストーリーのキーワードを使って例文を作ってみましょう。

Words from the story ストーリーのキーワード

- **Depression**
  うつ病

- **Suicide**
  自殺

- **Mental Hospital**
  精神病院

- **Blackmail**
  脅す

Key Word_01

Depression うつ病

Utsubyou

Koji has fallen into a deep depression after finding out he was impotent.

浩司は勃起不全ということがわかり、重度のうつ病になってしまった。

Koji ha bokki fuzen toiu koto ga wakari, jyuudo no utsubyou ni natte shimatta.

Key Word_02

Suicide <u>自殺</u>
Jisatsu

If someone with multiple personalities threatens to commit suicide, is that considered a hostage crisis?

自殺志願者が多重人格の人だったら、それは人質事件になるの？

Jisatsu shigansha ga tajyuu jinkaku no hito dattara, sore wa hitojichi jiken ni naru no?

Key Word_03

Mental Hospital <u>精神病院</u>
Seishinbyouin

The mental hospital houses all the crazies and weirdos.

精神病院にはイカれた奴と危険人物がいるところなんだ。

Seishinbyoin ni wa ikareta yatsu to kikenjinbutsu ga iru tokoro nan da.

Key Word_04

Blackmail <u>脅す</u>
Odosu

If you can't get what you want from life, you can always try blackmail.

自分の人生で欲しい物が手に入らないならば、脅して手に入れてみたら？
※もちろん、それはダメですよ。

jibun no jinsei de hoshi mono ga te ni haranai naraba, odoshite te ni irete mitara?

CHAPTER 2 Ann's Life Scenario 2 　　CD トラック 06

1: **Hit me with a double this time.**
こんどはダブルで。
Kondo ha daburu de.

3: **Don't tell me what to do bitch!**
命令するんじゃねーよ、クソ女。
Meirei surunja ne yo, kuso onna

5: **I'm sorry Ann, it's just, I found out I'm impotent.**
アンちゃんごめんね、実は最近インポって分かってさ。
Anchan gomen ne, jitsu ha saikin inpo tte wakatte sa.

7: **Thanks.**
ありがとう。
Arigatou.

Ann's Life Scenario 2
アンの人生シナリオ2「クラブ若葉で」
コージがアンの経営するホステスクラブに来店した。

2: I think you've had enough Koji.
コージ、飲み過ぎなんだから、もういいんじゃない。
Kōji, nomi suginan dakara, mō īn janai.

4: What the fuck Koji, what is your problem?
なによコージ、なんか文句あるわけ？
Nani yo Koji, nanka monku aru wake?

6: Oh my! So you can only shoot blanks? Ok, next one's on the house.
あらま！ ほぼ種なしなのね？
わかった、次は店のおごりよ。
Ara ma! Hobo tane nashina no ne?
Wakatta, tsugi wa mise no ogori yo.

Important Phrases 重要なフレーズ

※ **Double** ダブル Daburu
お酒のショット2杯分のこと。 Two shots of alcohol.

※ **Impotent** 勃起不全 Bokkifuzen
女性を妊娠させられない状態のこと。 When you cannot impregnate a woman.

※ **On the house** 店のおごり Mise no ogori
俗語でフリードリンクやサービスを指す。 A slang term for free drinks or services

CHAPTER 2 What a hostess or mama-san would say...

Ann-What a hostess or mama-san would say...

クラブのママ、アンが言う黄金フレーズ10

使うのに注意= ☠　注意= ☠☠　かなり危険= ☠☠☠

Phrase_01
Being sexy is our job!
美しくいることがアタシたちの仕事よ。
Utsukushiku iru koto ga atashi tachi no shigoto yo.

Phrase_02
Boob grabs are common in this line of work.
オッパイを触られるぐらいのことは、この仕事では当たり前よ。
Oppai wo sawarareru gurai no koto wa kono shigoto de wa atarimae yo.

Phrase_03 ☠
If you go too far, I'll punch you in the dick.
おさわりしすぎたら股間をパンチよ。
Osawari shisugitara kokan wo panchi yo.

Phrase_04
Let's sing karaoke and forget about our troubles!
一日の疲れを忘れてカラオケで歌いましょう。
Ichini no tsukare wo wasurete karaoke de utaimashou.

Phrase_05
You can look, but don't touch.
見てもいいけど、おさわりはダメよ。
Mitemo iikedo osawari wa dame yo.

Phrase_06
You might be the most boring person I have ever met.
私のこれまでの人生で会った中であなたが一番つまらない男ね。

Watashi no koremade no jinsei atta naka de anata ga ichiban tsumaranai otoko ne.

Phrase_07
Let's do body shots!
ボディーショットやろう！

Bodi shotto yaro!

Phrase_08
Do you think I'm sexy?
私ってセクシー？

Watashi tte sekushi?

Phrase_09
Milfs are totally trending right now.
いま、時代は熟女よ。

Ima, jidai wa jukujo yo.

Phrase_10
My favorite boyfriend is rechargeable.
私の一番の彼氏はバイブ（大人のおもちゃ）よ。

Watashi no ichiban no kareshi wa baibu yo.

※Phrase_07: Bodyshotsは胸にショットグラスをはさんで相手にお酒を飲ませること。

※Phrase_09: 熟女を示すmilfsは、Mother I'd Like To Fuckを省略した語。

※Phrase_10: 再充電可能という意味のrechargeableは、大人のおもちゃを指す隠語。

Koji-What a customer says...
アンのクラブに来る お客さん（コージ）が言うフレーズ10

使うのに注意＝☠ 注意＝☠☠ かなり危険＝☠☠☠

Phrase_01
I think I have a boner.
オレ、勃起してるかも。
Ore bokki shiteru kamo

Phrase_02 ☠
Are your boobs real?
お前のオッパイ本物か？
Omae no oppai honmono ka?

Phrase_03
Your hair is soft like my moms.
お前の髪は、オレの母ちゃんのみたいに柔らかいな。
Omae no kami wa ore no kachan no mitai ni yawarakai na.

Phrase_04
※
Put it on my tab.
つけといて。
Tsuketoite.

Phrase_05 ☠☠
Can I squeeze your tit?
オッパイつまんでいい？
Oppai tsumande ii?

Phrase_06
Are you warming up the chair until the cute girls come.
お前は可愛い子が来るまで席をあっためてるだけだよな？
Omae wa kawaii ko ga kuru made seki wo attameteru dake dayo na?

Phrase_07 ☠
I didn't know I would be paying by the hour to talk to ugly bitches.
こんなブサイクな奴らと話すのに毎時間金を払うなんて思わなかったぜ。
Konna busaiku na yatsura to hanasu no ni mai jikan ni kane wo haru nante omowanakatta ze.

Phrase_08
I thought you were attractive, but then you opened your mouth.
キミは魅力的だと思ったけど、話し出すと微妙だな。
Kimi wa miryokuteki da to omottakedo, hanashi dasu to bimyou dana.

Phrase_09
You are more persistent than the TV debt collector!
お前はテレビの集金の奴よりしつこいな！
Omae wa terebi no shukin no yatsu yori shitsukoi na!

Phrase_10 ☠☠☠
You better hope you marry rich.
お前は金持ちと結婚しろよ。
Omae wa kanemochi to kekkon shiro yo.

※Phrase_04: Put it on my tab.は、クレジットカードで請求をしてくれという意味。
※Phrase_06: 隣の席に座っている好みではない女の子に対して席を空けて欲しい事をほのめかしている。
※Phrase_08: 相手に対しての印象が悪かったときに使う。
※Phrase_10: 人間的に魅力がなく、金ぐらいしか救う方法がない人に対しての言葉。これを聞いたときは要注意！
※Phrase_02、05、06、07は女の子に殴られる覚悟で言おう。

CHAPTER 2 Helpful Words And Phrases GOOD & BAD

シナリオに関連する単語を使ったGOODとBADフレーズ

Helpful Words And Phrases
GOOD & BAD

All you can drink 飲み放題 Nomihodai

GOOD
The last time we had all you can drink, I woke up in a dumpster.
この前飲み放題に行ったとき、目が覚めたらゴミ箱の中にいた。
kono mae nomihoudai ni itta toki, me ga sametara gomi bako no naka ni ita.

BAD
Take him to an all you can drink, get him wasted, then rob him of his money.
奴を飲み放題に連れて、ぐでんぐでんにして金品巻き上げちまえ。
Yatsu wo nomihoudai ni tsurete, kudenguden ni shite kinpin makiage chimae.

Whiskey ウイスキー Uisuki

GOOD
Whiskey is a great drink that mixes well with many types of alcohol.
ウイスキーはほかの酒となんでも混ぜられるいい酒だ。
Uisuki wa hokano sake to nandemo mazerareru ii sake da.

BAD
Whiskey and coke goes well together, but whiskey and cocaine goes even better!
ウイスキーとコーラって合うんだよな、でもウイスキーとコカインならもっといいぜ！
Uisuki to kora tte aun dayo na, demo uisuki to kokain nara motto ii ze!

Beautiful 美しい Utsukushi

GOOD
Your mom is far more beautiful than you.
キミのお母さんの方がキミよりずっと美しい。
kimi no okasan no hou ga kimi yori zutto utsukishi.

BAD
She was beautiful when I took her home last night...not so much anymore.
昨日の夜うちに連れて来たとき、彼女はきれいだったんだけどな……でももう、そうでもなくなっちまった。
kinou no yoru uchi ni tsurete kita toki, kanojo wa kirei dattan dakedo na... demo mou, soudemo naku nacchimatta.

Bring another おかわり Okawari

GOOD
Bring me another beer, this one is warm.
これぬるくなってるからビールのおかわりをくれ。
Kore nuruku natteru kara biru no okawari wo kure.

BAD
Tell the mama-san to bring another girl, this one is butt ugly!
ママさんにほかの女の子を連れてくるように頼んでよ、こいつ、すっげーブスだから！
Mamasan ni hoka no onannko wo tsurete kuru youni tanondeyo, koitsu, sugge busu dakara!

CHAPTER 3

EMI ITO
伊藤エミ

Emi Ito's Life Story
伊藤エミの人生

10年後、エミは24歳になりました。
学業優秀だった彼女の人生はどうなったのか見てみましょう。

Emi's Life Story

For a time Emi had everything going for her, a full ride into one of the best medical universities in the country, and a promising career in medicine. One summer night all that changed when she cheated on Mike Davis with Billie Green, causing a fallout of friends on all sides. She began to drink and then later take drugs for comfort, throwing her future out the window. Turning next to prostitution to help support her new habit. Now she works at Ms.Green's Club Wakaba to make ends meet.

かつての絵美は、順風満帆な人生を送っていた。有名国立医大へ進学し、医師としての将来も約束されていた。ある夏の夜、ビリー・グリーンとの浮気がきっかけで彼氏だったマイク・デイビスを裏切ったことから、あらゆる方面の友達と縁が切れて、すべてが変わってしまった。お酒を始めたのちに、癒しを求めて麻薬にも走り、自分の未来を窓から投げ捨ててしまった。また新たな遊び代のために、カラダを売るようになっていった。そして今は、日々の生活費用を稼ぐために、グリーン先生のクラブ若葉で働くようになった。

Katsute no Emi wa, junpūmanpan'na jinsei wo okutte ita. Yūmei kokuritsu idai e shingaku shi, ishi to shite no shōrai mo yakusoku sarete ita. Aru natsu noyoru, Biri Gurin to no uwaki ga kikkake de kareshidatta Maiku Deibisu wo uragitta koto kara, arayuru hōmen no tomodachi to en ga kirete, subete ga kawatte shimatta. Osake wo hajimeta nochi ni, iyashi wo motomete mayaku ni mo hashiri, jibun no mirai wo mado kara nagesutete shimatta. Mata aratana asobi-dai no tame ni, karada wo uru yō ni natte itta. Soshite ima wa, hibi no seikatsu hiyō wo kasegu tame ni, Gurīn sensei no kurabu Wakaba de hataraku yō ni natta.

I always use lube, it makes awkward situations nice and smooth. Whether he is having trouble getting it in, or you are having trouble getting excited, never leave home without it!

なんでもナイスでスムーズにするために、私はいつもローションを使うの。たとえば、挿入しにくいときや興奮するのが難しいときでも困らないよう、常に持ち歩いているのよ。

Nan demo naisu de sumūzu ni suru tame ni, watashi wa itsumo rōshon wo tsukau no. Tatoeba, sōnyū shinikui toki ya kōfun suru no ga muzukashī toki demo komaranai yō, tsune ni mochiaruiteiru no yo.

CHAPTER 3 Words from the story used in phrases

Words from the story used in phrases

物語の単語を使って文を作る

エミの人生ストーリーのキーワードを使って例文を作ってみましょう。

Words from the story　ストーリーのキーワード

Cheated
浮気

Fallout
縁がきれる

Prostitution
売春

Habit
遊び(癖)

Key Word_01

Cheated 浮気

Uwaki

The man cheated on his wife constantly.

その男は妻がいるのにいつも浮気してる。

Sono otoko wa tsuma ga iru no ni itsumo uwaki shiteru.

Key Word_02

Fallout 縁が切れる
En ga kireru

I had a falling out with my family after being arrested for groping girls on the train.

電車で痴漢して捕まってから家族との縁が切れた。

Densha demo chikanshite tsukamatte kara kazoku to no en ga kireta.

Key Word_03

# Prostitution 売春（をする）
Baishun(wo suru)

If soliciting prostitution is bad, then I am a very bad boy.

もし売春の勧誘をすることが悪いんだったら、オレは相当悪い男だ。

Moshi baishun no kanyuu wo suru koto ga waruin dattara, ore wa soutou warui otoko da.

Key Word_04

# Habit 遊び（癖）
Asobi(kuse)

I have a habit of sticking a finger up my butt when I wipe.

お尻を拭くときに、よくお尻の穴に指を入れる遊び（癖）がある。

Oshiri wo fuku toki ni, yoku oshiri no ana ni yubi wo ireru asobi(kuse) ga aru.

CHAPTER 3 Emi's Life Scenario 3 | CD トラック 10

Emi's Life Scenario 3
エミの人生シナリオ3「ラブホテルにて」

慎はエミをホテルに呼んだ。

1: Oh yeah baby, who is your daddy?
ベイビー、パパと呼べよ。
Beibī, papa to yobeyo.

3: What do you mean? Can't you tell I'm hitting your ovaries!
どういう意味だよ？
子宮（卵巣）にあたってんの
わからないのか？
Douiu imi dayo? Shikyu(ransou) ni atatten no wakaranai no ka?

2: Huh? Did you start yet?
えっ？もう始まってるの？
E? Mou hajimatteruno?

4: Did you stick it in already? I can't feel anything.
もう入れた？ なにも感じないけど。
Mou ireta? Nani mo kanjinai kedo.

Important Phrases 重要なフレーズ

※ **Who is your daddy**　フー イズ ユア ダディ
セックスしているときに言葉攻めでよく使われるフレーズ。
A phrase often used during sex to show authority over the woman.

※ **Stick it in**　スティック イット イン
ペ●スを挿入すること。 Insert your penis into another person.

※ **Ovaries**　オヴァリー
卵子を産む女性の性器名のこと。 The name of the organ in a woman where eggs are produced.

CHAPTER 3 What would a prostitute say...

CD トラック 11

Emi -What would a prostitute say...

売春婦エミが言うお決まりフレーズ10

使うのに注意=☠　注意=☠☠　かなり危険=☠☠☠

Phrase_01
Did you bring a jimmy/rubber/condom?
ゴム持ってきた？
Gomu mottekita?

Phrase_02 ☠☠
I like it raw.
ナマでやるのが好き。
Nama de yaru no ga suki.

Phrase_03
You've got ten minutes left.
あと10分ね。
Ato Juppun ne.

Phrase_04
You have to shower first.
先にシャワー浴びてきて。
Saki ni shawa abite kite.

Phrase_05 ☠☠
I don't do any kinky※ shit.
変態なことはしないから。
Hentai na koto wa shinai kara.

Phrase_06
I wanted to be treated with ※respect.
敬意をもって接してくんない？

Keii wo motte sesshite kunnai?

Phrase_07
Are you a cop?
警官じゃないわよね？

Keikan jyanaiwayo ne?

Phrase_08
I'm not that kind of girl.
私はそんな女じゃないから。

Watashi wa sonna onna jyanai kara.

Phrase_09 ☠☠☠
※Herpes, gonorrhea, syphilis you name it, I got it.
ヘルペス、淋病、梅毒、そのほかなんでも言って。（私持っているけど大丈夫よね）

Herupesu, rinbyou, baidoku, sono hoka nandemo itte.

Phrase_10
Did you just yell out, Mom?
さっき「ママ」と叫んでた？（このマザコンが！）

Sakki "mama" to sakendeta?

※Phrase_05: kinkyは、変なという意味で使われますが、性的な要求の場合は、異常な意味があるときに使われます。言われたら要注意。

※Phrase_06: 女性はいつでも女として丁寧に接して欲しいもの。

※Phrase_09: このフレーズを言うとお客はどん引きします。あなたのパートナーを脅す場合を除き、あなたの持っている性病を自慢しない方がよい。

CHAPTER 3 What to say to a hooker...
CD トラック 12

Emi -What to say to a hooker...
売春婦エミのお客に言われたフレーズ10

使うのに注意=☠ 注意=☠☠ かなり危険=☠☠☠

Phrase_01 ☠☠☠
How much for a blowjob/handjob/fuck?
一回いくら?
Ikkai ikura?

Phrase_02
Have you been tested?
検査は済んでいるよな?
Kensa wa sunde iruyona?

Phrase_03 ☠
Where is your pimp?
おまえのぽん引き(売春婦を斡旋する人)はどこだ?
Omae no pon biki wa doko da?

Phrase_04
Can we wrap this up, I have to pick up my kids.
早く終わらせてくんないかな、子供たちを迎えに行かなければならないんだから。
Hayaku owarasetekunnai kana, kodomotachi wo mukae ni ikanakereba naranain dakara.

Phrase_05
Do you have any 5 minute specials?
5分間でなにか特別にできることある?
5 Funkan de nani ka tokubetsu ni dekiru koto aru?

Phrase_06 ☠☠
Do you do group discounts?
団体割引してる？

Dantai waribiki shiteru?

Phrase_07 ☠☠
I could remove 90 percent of your beauty with a wet nap.
キミの美しさの90％はウエットティッシュで取れちゃうね。
（厚化粧のため、化粧を取ったらほぼブスという意味）

Kimi no usukushisa no 90% wa uetto tisshu de torechau ne.

Phrase_08
※
Your makeup looks like it was applied with a shotgun.
キミのメークって、ショットガンでつけたみたいだね。

Kimi no mēkutte ha shottogan de tsuketa mitai dane.

Phrase_09 ☠
You may not be the best looking girl, but beauty is only a light switch away!
キミはすごくキレイなわけじゃないけど、
美しさはスイッチひとつで明かりを消すだけの問題だよ！

Kimi wa sugoku kirei na wake janaikedo, utsukushi-sa wa suicchi hitotsu de akari wo kesu dake no mondai dayo!

Phrase_10
I'll never forget the first time we met, but I'll keep trying.
キミに初めて会ったときを忘れたいのに、忘れられないよ。

Kimi ni hajimete atta toki wo wasuretai no ni, wasurerarenai yo.

> ※Phrase_01: このフレーズをいきなり使うのは要注意。殴られるのを覚悟で使おう。ちなみにblowjobは、フェラチオ。handjobは手こき、マスターベーション、fuckは、性交のこと。
>
> ※Phrase_02: ここでの検査は性病の検査と言う。
>
> ※Phrase_04: やる気が出ないほどブサイクが来た場合に使う。また早く終わらせたいときは、仕上げるという意味のwrap upを使う。
>
> ※Phrase_08: ショットガンで打ったようにメークが厚く下手という意味がある。

CHAPTER 3 Helpful Words And Phrases GOOD & BAD

シナリオに関連する単語を使ったGOODとBADフレーズ

Helpful Words And Phrases
GOOD & BAD

Condom コンドーム Kondomu

GOOD
Oh no, I think the condom broke!
あぁしまった、コンドームが破れた!
Aashimatta, kondomu ga yabureta!

BAD
I bet you thought I was going to wear a condom, I lied!
オレがコンドームつけると思っただろ、ウソだったんだよ!
Ore ga kondomu tsukeru to omotta daro, uso dattan dayo!

Blowjob フェラチオ Ferachio

GOOD
If you are going to give a good blow job, please be wary of your teeth.
もし上手いフェラチオをするつもりなら、歯には気をつけてね。
Moshi umai ferachio wo suru tsumori nara, ha ni wa ki wo tsukete ne.

BAD
If you can't give a good blowjob, I hope you like being single!
もし上手なフェラチオができないんなら、きっと独身でいるのがいいんだろうな!
Moshi jozu na ferachio ga dekinain nara, kitto dokushin deiru no ga iin darou na!

Anal sex アナルセックス Anaru sekkusu

GOOD
Every couple should try experimenting with anal sex at least once.
カップル皆一度は、アナルセックスを経験してみるべきだ。
Kappuru minna ichido wa, anaru sekkusu wo keikenshite miru beki da.

BAD
If they find anal sex painful and you are out of lube, tell them it wouldn't hurt if they loved you more.
もしアナルセックスが痛くて、ローションもないっていうんなら、もっとやれば痛くなくなるって言ってやれ。
Moshi anarusekkusu ga itakute, rōshon mo nai tte iu nara, motto yareba itakunaku naru tte itte yare.

The Pill ピル Piru

GOOD
Taking the pill is her responsibility.
ピルを飲むのは、彼女の義務だ。
Piru wo nomu no wa, kanojo no gimu da.

BAD
You should have told me you were off the pill before I blew my load!
ピルを飲んでないんなら、出しちまう前に言えよ!
Piru wo nondenain nara, dashichau mae ni ieyo!

Fuck my life.
人生くそくらえ

I just want to make the pain stop.
この痛みを止めたいだけなのよ

I don't do anything for free.
お金くれるならなんでもやるわ

Talk to the hand!
もういいわ

You're such a n00b!
お前って初心者だな!

You call yourself a man !?
それでも男!?

Get outta my face, I'll mess you up!
消えろ、さもないとボッコボコにするぞ

You are no match for me!
わたしにはかなわないね

Fabulous!
すてき!

What the fuck you looking at punk?
なに見てんだよ?

CHAPTER 4

JUDY BROWN
ジュディ・ブラウン

Judy Brown's Life Story
ジュディ・ブラウンの人生

日本に留学していたジュディにも生活に変化がありました。
どんな人生を送っているか見てみましょう。

Judy's Life Story

Judy had high hopes of becoming a singer one day. But her **risque** sexual behavior and late night **gangbangs** got her involved with a married man. After a **scandalous** failed pregnancy with Bin dashed her hopes of signing a record contract, she began working two jobs. Now a jarred, self-centered girl with a false sense of entitlement, she hopes to save enough money to eventually escape this **dump**.

ジュディは将来歌手になることを強く望んでいたが、彼女の**キワドイ**性癖と夜の**乱交**パーティー三昧の中で、ひとりの既婚者にハマってしまった。そしてビンとの**過ち**から妊娠をしたことによって、彼女の歌手としてレコード会社と契約するという夢に終止符が打たれてしまった。ショックを受けた彼女は資金さえ貯めればこの**ごたごた**がすべて解決されるという見当違いな望みをもって2つの仕事を始めたのだった。

Judi wa shōrai kashu ni naru koto wo tsuyoku nozondeita ga, kanojo no kiwadoi seiheki to yoru no rankō pātī zanmai no naka de, hitori no kikon-sha ni hamatte shimatta. Soshite Bin to no ayamachi kara ninshin wo shita koto ni yotte, kanojo no kashu to shite rekōdo kaisha to keiyaku suru to iu yume ni shūshifu ga utarete shimatta. Shokku wo uketa kanojo wa shikin sae tamereba kono gotagota ga subete kaiketsu sareru to iu kentō chigaina nozomi wo motte futatsu no shigoto wo hajimeta no datta.

Whatever I have to do to make some money and get out of this shithole, I will. Whatever you do, don't order the largest-size, sweet coffee drink. There are enough calories and sugar in there to make you fatter than me.

金を稼いでこのクソみたいな状況から抜け出せるなら絶対になんだってするわ。なにがあろうと一番大きいサイズの甘口コーヒーは注文しないで。あんたを私よりデブらせるのに十分なカロリーと砂糖が入ってるわよ。

Kane wo kaseide kono kuso mitaina jōkyō kara nukedaserunara zettai ni nan datte suru wa. Nani ga arou to ichiban ōkī saizu no amakuchi kōhī wa chūmon shinaide. Anta wo watashi yori deburaseru noni jūbun'na karorī to satō ga haitteru wa yo.

CHAPTER 4 Words from the story used in phrases

Words from the story used in phrases

物語の単語を使って文を作る

ジュディの人生ストーリーのキーワードを使って例文を作ってみましょう。

Words from the story ストーリーのキーワード

Risque
際どい

Gangbangs
乱交パーティー

Scandalous
過ち

Dump
ごたごた

Key Word_01

Risque 際どい

Kiwadoi

After a few drinks, she is known to take off her top and get a little risque.

彼女は少しお酒を飲むだけで、脱いでエッチ(際どく)になることで知られている。

Kanojo wa sukoshi osake wo nomu dake de, nuide etchi ni naru koto de shirarete iru.

Key Word_02

Gangbangs 乱交パーティー
Rankoupati

Gangbangs are common in adult videos, but I have trouble just getting one person to join me.

アダルトビデオでは乱交パーティーは一般的にやっているが、自分だと、ひとり誘うだけでも難しい。

Adarutobideo dewa, rankō pātī wa ippanteki ni yatte iru ga, jibun dato, hitori sasou dake demo muzukashī.

Key Word_03

Scandalous 過ち
Ayamachi

The politician's nude photos in UN offices surfaced on the internet and caused an international scandal.

国連のオフィスから政治家のヌード写真がインターネットを通じて明るみになると国際的な問題に発展していった。

Kokuren no ofisu kara seijika no nūdo shashin ga intānetto wo tsūjite akarumi ni naru to kokusai tekina mondai ni hatten shite itta.

Key Word_04

Dump ごたごた
Gotagota

Her house is a dump, her family is in tatters, and she has no money.

彼女の家はごたごたしている。家庭は崩壊しちゃって彼女は一文無しだ。

Kanojo no ie wa gotagota shite iru. Katei wa hōkai shichatte kanojo wa ichimonnashi da.

CHAPTER 4 Judy's Life Scenario 4 — CD トラック14

Judy's Life Scenario 4
ジュディの人生シナリオ4「コーヒーショップ」

ジュディは客のビリーに対して横柄な態度をとる。

1: I said no whip on my coffee three times, you dumb bitch.

3回もクリームを入れんなって言ってんだろう、クソビッチ!
Sankai mo kurimu wo irenna tte itten darou, kuso bicchi!

3: Skank!

このブス!!!
Kono busu!

5: I have never been so insulted!

本当に失礼だわ。
Hontou ni shitsurei da wa!

2: Who are you calling a bitch, bitch!

誰のことをビッチと呼んでんのよ！ビッチ！

Dare no koto wo bicchi to yonden noyo! bicchi!

4: Talk to the hand!

もういいわ。もう黙りなさいよ!

Mou ii wa. Mou damarinasaiyo!

Important Phrases　重要なフレーズ

※ Skank　スカンク
汚い女性や乱れた女に使う侮辱的な言葉。
An insulting term that means the woman is unkept or dirty.

※ Talk to the hand　トーク トゥ ザ ハンド
失礼な会話の終わらせ方、口論に飽れたときに使う。
A rude way to end a conversation, when the person is fed up with arguing.

Judy - What would a coffee shop barista say...

性格の悪いバリスタ、ジュディが言うフレーズ10

使うのに注意=☠ 注意=☠☠ かなり危険=☠☠☠

Phrase_01
I'm sorry, we don't sell alcoholic coffee drinks here.

ごめんなさいねー。ここでは、アルコール入りコーヒーは売っていません。

Gomennasai. Kokode wa, arukoru iri kohi wa utteimasen.

Phrase_02
One organic coffee, for the giant hippy.

あのマジヒッピーな人にオーガニックコーヒーをひとつ。

Ano maji hippi na hito ni oganikku kohi wo hitotsu,

Phrase_03 ☠☠
Stop hogging all the outlets, go back to your own shit apartment.

豚みたいにアウトレット商品をほじくり返すのはやめて自分のクソみたいな家に帰れよ。

Buta mitai ni autoretto shōhin wo hojikuri kaesu no wa yamete jibun no kuso mitaina ie ni kaereyo!!!

Phrase_04
Awww you burned your hand? Next time use a lid!

あー、手をやけどしちゃった？次はフタを使いな！

Aa, te wo yakedo shichatta? Tsugi wa futa wo tsukai na!

Phrase_05
If you want a larger size, you may need a bucket!

もっと大きいサイズ欲しければ、バケツが必要だよ。

Motto okii saizu hoshikereba, baketsu ga hitsuyou dayo.

Phrase_06 💀💀💀
You look like shit, I'll make that espresso a double.
ひどい姿だな。エスプレッソをダブルで作ってあげるよ。

Hidoi sugata da na. Esupuresso wo daburu de tsukutte ageru yo.

Phrase_07
You need more than a morning coffee, you need a complete make-over.※
朝のコーヒーより、化粧し直すのが必要だな。

Asa no kōhī yori, keshō shinaosu no ga hitsuyō dana.

Phrase_08 💀💀💀
You are way too fat to be drinking this sugary drink.
この甘ったるいドリンクを飲むにはお前はデブ過ぎ。

Kono amattarui dorinku wo nomu no ni wa omae wa debusugi.

Phrase_09 💀
We are not overpriced, you are just poor!
コーヒーの値段が高い訳じゃなくて、ただお前が貧乏なだけだよ!!

Kohi no nedan ga takai wake janakute, tada omae ga binbou nan dayo!

Phrase_10
Drink coffee! Do stupid things faster with more energy!
コーヒー飲めよ! エネルギーつけて早くバカみたいなことをやれよ。

Kohi nomeyo! Enerugi tsukete hayaku baka mitai na koto wo yare yo.

※Phrase_02: でかいヒッピーではなく、マジにヒッピーをやっている人のことを言う。最近では、軽蔑的な表現として使うようになっている。また怠け者という意味もある。

※Phrase_03: hoggingは、なにかを独り占めするときに使います。ここではアウトレット商品ですが、ほか食べ物、毛布などにも使う。

※Phrase_07: a complete make-over.は、見た目の改善が必要という意味。

CHAPTER 4　What would a customer at a coffee shop say...

CD トラック **16**

Billie -What would a customer at a coffee shop say...

性格の悪いバリスタ、ジュディに使うお客（ビリー）のフレーズ10

使うのに注意＝☠　　注意＝☠☠　　かなり危険＝☠☠☠

Phrase_01 ☠☠

This coffee tastes like shit!

このコーヒークソみたいな味だな!
Kono kohi kuso mitai na aji da na!

Phrase_02 ☠☠☠

How many third world countries did you exploit for this coffee?

このコーヒーのために、どのくらいの発展途上国から搾取した?
Kono kohi no tameni, donogurai no hatten tojoukoku kara sakushu shita?

Phrase_03 ☠☠

These coffee beans smell like ass.

このコーヒー豆、くせぇな。（ケツの穴みたいな匂いがするw）
Kono kōhī mame, kuse na.

Phrase_04

This coffee is more expensive than my train fare!

このコーヒーは、オレの電車代より高いな!
Kono kohi wa ore no densha dai yori takai na!

Phrase_05

I am just not ready to start the day until my 9th cup.

9杯飲まないと、1日が始まらない。
9-Hai nomanai to, ichinichi ga hajimaranai.

Phrase_06
This espresso wouldn't fill a thimble.
このエスプレッソは、指ぬきよりも少ないな。

Kono esupuresso wa, yubinuki yorimo sukunaina

Phrase_07
No pets allowed? Then how did you get in?
ペット禁止？ じゃあお前はどうやって入ったんだよ？

Petto kinshi? Jaa omae dou yatte haittan dayo?

Phrase_08
I don't speak Italian, just gimme the big one.
イタリア語は話せないけど、とりあえずそのでかいのちょうだい。

Itaria-go wa hanasenaikedo, toriaezu sono dekai no choudai.

Phrase_09
If your coffee is as bad as your wifi, I'll pass.
お前のコーヒーがお前のWi-Fiと同じぐらいダメだったら、オレは要らない。

Omae no kōhī ga omae no waifai to onaji gurai dame dattara, ore wa iranai.

Phrase_10
Yeah, can I get a cafe au lait, hold the coffee.
うん。コーヒー抜きのカフェオレちょうだい。

Un. Kohi nuki no kafe ore choudai.

※Phrase_06：thimble（指ぬき）は、縫い物するときに使う指の１関節ぐらいのカップ状のこと。量が少ないという意味。

※Phrase_08：エスプレッソやカプチーノなどのメニュー名はイタリア語なので、意味はわからないけど、とにかく大きいのを欲しいと言う場合に使う。

※Phrase_09：店のWifi接続が不良ならあまり信用できない店なのでコーヒーの品質もきっと悪いという意味。

※Phrase_10：コーヒーなしのカフェオレを注文したら、ミルクしかもらえない。

CHAPTER 4 Helpful Words And Phrases GOOD & BAD

シナリオに関連する単語を使ったGOODとBADフレーズ
Helpful Words And Phrases
GOOD & BAD

Sugar 砂糖 Satou

GOOD
I wish there was a sugar free version of soda that actually tasted good.
本当においしい砂糖無添加のソーダがあればいいのにな。
Hontou ni oishi satou mutenka no soda ga areba ii no ni na.

BAD
Sugar free anything tastes like shit.
砂糖無添加は、どれもクソまずい。
Satou mutenka ha dore mo kuso mazui.

Soy milk 豆乳 Tounyuu

GOOD
Vegetarians and hippies love soy milk.
ベジタリアンとヒッピーは、豆乳が好きだ。
Bejitarian to hippi ha, tounyuu ga suki da.

BAD
Keep your organic hippie soy milk away from my coffee bitch!
オーガニックのヒッピー豆乳なんて、オレのコーヒーに近づけるんじゃねえよ!
Oganikku no hippi tounyuu nante, ore no kohi ni chikatzukerun jyane yo!

Overpriced 高すぎる値段 Takasugiru nedan

GOOD
The price of this coffee may be overpriced, but I am rich so it doesn't matter.
コーヒーの値段が高すぎるけど、オレは金持ちだから関係ないね。
Kōhī no nedan ga takasugiru kedo, ore wa kanemochidakara kankeinai ne.

BAD
I didn't become filthy rich by giving my money away to charity or paying for overpriced goods!
オレがめちゃ金持ちになったのは、チャリティーやバカ高い値段のグッズに金を払うためなんかじゃないぜ!
Ore ga mecha kanemochi ni natta no wa, charitī ya baka takai nedan no guzzu ni kane wo harau tame janai ze!

Child Labor 未成年労働 Miseinen roudou

GOOD
Coffee beans come from many third world countries where laws against child labor are not enforced.
コーヒー豆が作られている多くの発展途上国では、未成年労働を取り締まる法律は徹底されていない。
Kohi mame ga tsukurareteiru ooku no hatten toujoukoku de wa, misei nen roudou wo tori shimaru houritsu wa tattei sarete inai.

BAD
Your birth was an accident, I would put you to work if it weren't for these damn child labor laws!
てめえが生まれたのが災難だったのさ、未成年労働規制法なんてなけりゃ、働かせてやったのによ!
Teme ga umareta no ga sainan dattanosa, miseinen roudou kisei nante nakeriya, hatarakasete yatta no ni yo!

CHAPTER 5

KOJI ISHIKAWA

石川 コージ

Koji Ishikawa's Life Story
石川コージの人生

アンの姉のリサと離婚してからコージも45歳になりました。
どんな人生を送っているか見てみましょう。

Koji's Life Story

Koji was married to Lisa, but Koji's obsession with young women, led him to being caught having an affair with Judy Brown. Lisa promptly divorced him and kicked him out of the house. Koji now spends most of his time online on 2channel and auctions buying junior idol memorabilia. He has moved back into his parents house. While his parasite lifestyle has not been kind to his health, but overall he seems happier now than ever.

コージはリサと結婚していたが、若い女へ夢中になり、ジュディ・ブラウンとの不倫関係にはまってしまった。するとリサからさっさと離婚され、家を追い出されてしまったコージは今、1日のほとんどを2ちゃんねるとネットオークションでロリコンアイドルのグッズを買いあさることに費やしていた。実家で両親と暮らすすねかじり生活は決して健康的な生活ではないが、コージは今までの人生で一番幸せだった。

Kōji wa Risa to kekkon shite itaga, wakai on'na e muchū ni nari, Judi Buraun to no furin kankei ni hamatte shimatta. Suruto Risa kara sassato rikon sare, ie wo oidasarete shimatta Kōji wa ima, ichi-nichi no hotondo wo ni-channeru to nettoōkushon de rorikon'aidoru no guzzu wo kaiasaru koto ni tsuiyashite ita. Jikka de ryōshin to kurasu sunekajiri seikatsu wa kesshite kenkō-tekina seikatsude wa naiga, Kōji wa ima made no jinsei de ichiban shiawase datta.

Being an otaku is hard work. You have to surf the net a lot, steal women's panties, attend many idol concerts, and treat your digital girlfriend with respect.

オタクでいるのも楽じゃないよ。ネットサーフィンに下着ドロ、アイドルのコンサートにも行かなくちゃだし二次元の彼女のことも構ってあげなくちゃいけないからね。

Otaku de iru no mo raku janai yo. Nettosāfin ni shitagidoro, aidoru no konsāto ni mo ikanakuchadashi nijigen no kanojo no koto mo kamatte agenakucha ikenaikara ne.

CHAPTER 5 Words from the story used in phrases

Words from the story used in phrases

物語の単語を使って文を作る

浩司の人生ストーリーのキーワードを使って例文を作ってみましょう。

Words from the story　ストーリーのキーワード

Obsession
夢中

Affair
不倫

Promptly
さっさと、すぐ

Parasite Lifestyle
すねかじり生活

Key Word_01

Obsession 夢中

Muchuu

His obsession with little girls was his undoing.

彼の破滅のもとは、ロリータに夢中なことである。

Kare no hametsu nomoto wa, rorīta ni muchūna koto de aru.

Key Word_02
Affair <u>不倫</u>
Furin

Every married man suffers from the curse of one vagina. An affair is nature's way of bringing balance to the relationship.

既婚男の全員がマ○コがひとつ限定の呪いにかかる。不倫は、
夫婦関係のバランスを保つための自然な方法である。

Kikon otoko no zen'in ga ma ○ ko ga hitotsu gentei no noroi ni kakaru. Furin wa, fūfu kankei no baransu wo tamotsu tame no shizen'na hōhō de aru.
※表現は著者の考えによるものです。

Key Word_03
Promptly <u>さっさと、すぐ</u>
Sugu

He promptly gave the officer the finger after receiving a speeding ticket.

彼はスピード違反の切符を受け取ってすぐ警官にファックサインをした。

Kare wa supīdo ihan no kippu wo uketotte sugu keikan ni fakkusain o shita.

Key Word_04
Parasite Lifestyle <u>すねかじり生活</u>
Sunekajiri seikatsu

The easiest way to save money in Japan is to live a parasite lifestyle, till your parents kick you out of the house.

日本で最も簡単に貯金する方法は、両親から家を追い出されるまで
すねがじり生活を送ることである。

Nihon de mottomo kantan ni chokin suru hōhō wa, ryōshin kara ie wo oidasareru made sunekajiri seikatsu wo okuru koto de aru.

CHAPTER 5 Koji's Life Scenario 5 — CD トラック 18

Koji's Life Scenario 5
コージの人生シナリオ5「アイドルコンサートにて」

コージとマイクは人気アイドルコンサートへ行った。

1: Oh my god they are so cute!
わああ、めちゃ可愛いい〜
Waa, mecha kawaii

3: There is no way you will get past security. But I can do one better.
セキュリティーは絶対通れないけど、いいもんあるぜ。
Sekyuritī wa zettai tōrenaikedo, iimon aru ze.

5: I have some exclusive upskirts of the girls, only 500 yen a piece.
女の子のスカートのなかの盗撮限定写真がいくつかあるから、1枚500円でどう?
On'nanoko no sukāto no naka no tōsatsu gentei shashin ga ikutsu ka arukara, ichi mai 500-en de dou?

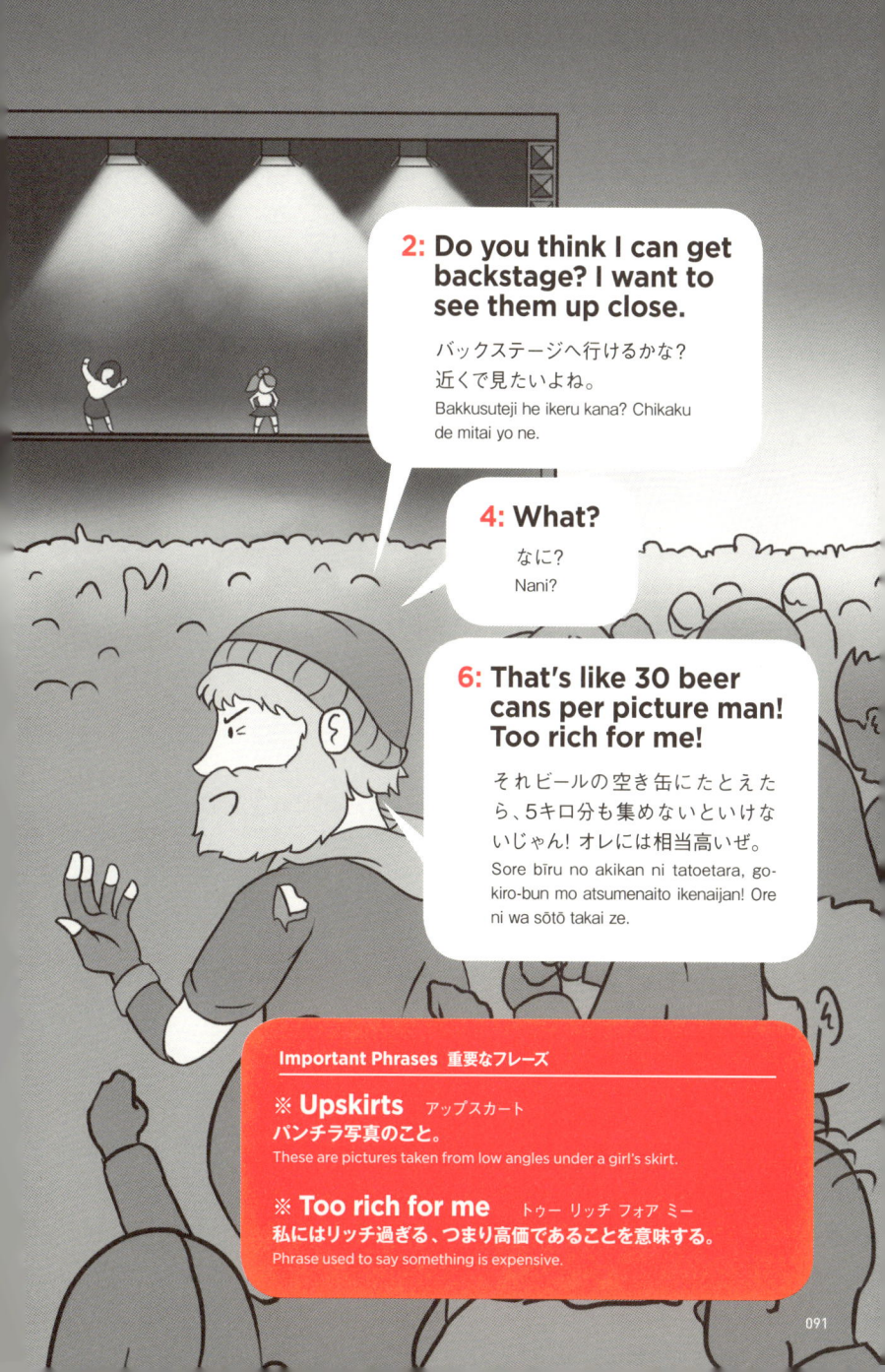

2: Do you think I can get backstage? I want to see them up close.

バックステージへ行けるかな？
近くで見たいよね。
Bakkusuteji he ikeru kana? Chikaku de mitai yo ne.

4: What?

なに？
Nani?

6: That's like 30 beer cans per picture man! Too rich for me!

それビールの空き缶にたとえたら、5キロ分も集めないといけないじゃん！オレには相当高いぜ。
Sore bīru no akikan ni tatoetara, go-kiro-bun mo atsumenaito ikenaijan! Ore ni wa sōtō takai ze.

Important Phrases 重要なフレーズ

※ **Upskirts** アップスカート
パンチラ写真のこと。
These are pictures taken from low angles under a girl's skirt.

※ **Too rich for me** トゥー リッチ フォア ミー
私にはリッチ過ぎる、つまり高価であることを意味する。
Phrase used to say something is expensive.

CHAPTER 5 — Things an otaku would say about or to an idol...

CD トラック **19**

Koji - Things an otaku would say about or to an idol...

アイドルオタク、コージのど定番フレーズ10

使うのに注意= ☠ 注意= ☠☠ かなり危険= ☠☠☠

Phrase_01 ☠
I like how her teeth point all different directions!
彼女のガタガタな歯並び具合が好き!
Kanojo no gatagatana hanarabi guai ga suki!

Phrase_02 ☠☠☠
I have a pair of her used panties.
彼女の使用済みパンツを持っているぜ。
Kanojo no shiyou zumi pantsu wo motteiru ze.

Phrase_03
I'm not a stalker, I'm just a concerned fan.
オレはストーカーじゃなくて、ただの関心のあるファンだ!
Ore wa sutoka jyanakute, tada no kannshin no aru fan da!

Phrase_04 ☠☠☠
I've been her fan since she was in elementary school!
オレは彼女が小学校にいるときからずっとファンだ。
Ore wa kanojo ga shogakkou ni iru toki kara zutto fan da.

Phrase_05
You're even hotter than Chun-Li!
あなたは、春麗(チュン・リー)よりずっとセクシーだ!
Anata wa Chun-Li yori zutto sekushi da!

Phrase_06
Will you sign my poster/cd/teddybear/game/t-shirt.
ポスター、CD、テディーベア、ゲーム、Tシャツにサインくれない？

Posuta, CD, tedeibea, gemu, teeshatsu, ni sain kurenai?

Phrase_07
Excuse me, but does this smell like chloroform to you?
すみません、これクロロホルムの匂いする？

Sumimasen, kore kurorohorumu no nioi suru?

Phrase_08
I love you like a fat kid loves cake.
デブの子供がケーキを愛してるように、愛してる。

Debu no kodomo ga keki wo aishiteru you ni, aishiteru.

Phrase_09
We went to the same elementary school, 20 years apart.
20年離れているけど、ボクたち同じ小学校に行ったんだよ。

20-nen hanareteirukedo bokutachi onaji shogakkou ni ittandayo.

Phrase_10
I'll never wash this hand again.
この手は一生洗わない。

Kono te wa ishou arawanai.

※Phrase_01: 一般的に日本では、crooked canine teeth（八重歯）は女性のチャームポイント。

※Phrase_03: オタクより優しい言い方はconcerned fanと言おう。

※Phrase_05: 春麗（チュン・リー）は、格闘ゲーム『ストリートファイター』に登場する女性格闘家。

Koji -Things an Idol may say to her otaku fans...

オタクのコージに対して、アイドルの気持ちフレーズ11

使うのに注意=☠　注意=☠☠　かなり危険=☠☠☠

Phrase_01
Please keep hand shakes to no more than 3 seconds.

3秒以上握手はしないでね。(ちなみに海外では握手会はあまりない。)

3-byou ijo akushu wa shinaide ne.

Phrase_02
I'm so pure, I actually piss rainbows and shit stars.

私は純粋だから、虹のオシッコと星のうんちをするの。

Watashi wa junsui dakara, niji no oshikko to hoshi no unchi wo suruno.

Phrase_03 ☠
I would love it if you didn't drip your sweat on me.

あなたの汗を私にたらさないでくれないかな。

Anata no ase wo watashi ni taranaide kurenai kana.

Phrase_04 ☠
I find you repulsive, but I love you as a fan.

あなたのことは気持ち悪いと思うけど、ファンとしては好きよ。

Anata no koto wa kimochi warui to omou kedo, fan toshite wa suki yo.

Phrase_05
I am actually not a virgin.

私、実はバージンじゃないのよ。

Watashi jitsu wa bājin jyanainoyo.

Phrase_06 ☠

I'm glad you worship me, because I really do look down upon you.

あなたを見下しているけど、ワタシを崇拝してくれるなら嬉しいわ。

Anata wo mikudashite irukedo, watashi wo sūhai shite kurerunara ureshī wa.

Phrase_07

Please stop following me.

つきまとわないで。

Tsukimatowanaide.

Phrase_08

Stop stalking me or I will punish you in the name of the moon. (Sailor Moon reference)

ストーカーしないで、さもないと月に代わってお仕置きよ。(セーラームーンの口調)

Sutoka shinaide, samonai to tsuki ni kawatte oshioki suru wayo.

Phrase_09

I'd appreciate it, if you stayed at least arms length away.

腕の長さぐらい離れてくれたら嬉しいわ。

Ude no nagasa gurai hanarete kuretara ureshi wa.

Phrase_10

I love my fans...to keep a 3 meter distance from me.

私は3メーターぐらいの距離を保つ……ファンが好き。

Watashi wa 3-metaru gurai no kyouri wo tamotsu… fan ga suki.

Phrase_11

If you really love me, you'll buy the Blu-ray box set.

もし私のことが好きなら、ブルーレイボックスのセットを買って。

Moshi watashi no koto ga suki nara, burrei bokkusu no setto wo katte.

※Phrase_04: repulsiveは不快でひどい表現なので、ファンとしては好きはうわべだけの言葉である。

CHAPTER 5 Helpful Words And Phrases GOOD & BAD

シナリオに関連する単語を使ったGOODとBADフレーズ

Helpful Words And Phrases
GOOD & BAD

Stalker ストーカー Sutoka

GOOD
I wasn't following her home, I was escorting her from a safe distance.
家まで彼女のあとをつけてたんじゃない、安全な距離をおいて、エスコートしてたんだ。
Ie made kanojo no ato wo tsuketanjanai, anzen'na kyori wo oite, esukōto shitetan da.

BAD
I am not her stalker. I am her boyfriend, I just haven't told her that yet.
オレはストーカーじゃない、彼女の恋人だ。ただ、まだそれを彼女に言ってないだけなんだ。
Ore wa sutoka jyanai, kanojo no koibito da. tada, mada sore wo kanojo ni ittenai dake nan da.

Pervert 変態 Hentai

GOOD
Some people say my collection of stolen women's panties makes me a pervert.
盗んだ女性下着のコレクションのことで、人はオレを変態と言う。
Nusunda josei shitagi no korekushon no koto de, hito wa ore wo hentai to iu.

BAD
Stop jerking off to pictures of underage girls, you pervert!
未成年の女の子の写真を見ながらマスターベーションをするんじゃない、この変態!
Miseinen no onna no ko no shashin wo minagara masutabeshon wo surunnjyanai, kono hentai!

Nerd オタク Otaku

GOOD
All he does is play video games and watch porn all day, what a nerd!
彼がすることは、テレビゲームで遊ぶのとポルノを見ることだけ。まったくなんてオタクだ!
Kare ga suru koto wa, terebigēmu de asobu no to poruno wo miru koto dake. Mattaku nante otaku da!

BAD
How does it feel to be a nerd and a virgin?
オタクで童貞の気分はどうだい?
Otaku de doutei no kibun wa doudai?

Mini skirt ミニスカート Minisukato

GOOD
Her skirt is so short, her butt cheeks keep peeking out to say hello to me.
彼女のスカートが短すぎて、半ケツがチラチラのぞかせてオレに挨拶をする。
Kanojo no sukāto ga mijika sugite, han ketsu ga chirachira nozokasete ore ni aisatsu wo suru.

BAD
Thank you for wearing such a short mini skirt, just bend over and give me easy access.
そんなに短いスカートをはいてくれてありがとう、ちょっとかがんでくれるかな? もっと見やすくなるんだけど。
Sonnani mijikai sukato wo haitekurete arigatou, chotto kagande kureru kana? motto miyasuku surun dake do.

CHAPTER 6

LISA GREEN
リサ・グリーン

Lisa Green's Life Story
リサ・グリーンの人生

コージとの離婚を経てリサは新しい人生を歩み始めました。
どんな人生を送っているか見てみましょう。

Lisa's Life Story

Lisa decided to give up on men after the Koji incident and come out as a lesbian to her best friend Kazuko; now the two are a couple. No longer having to conform to the traditional role of housewife, she has taken dramatic steps to live more true to herself. She's tough as nails and is quick not to let anyone forget that. She now works as a motorcycle mechanic at the garage Shin often visits to fix up his bike.

リサはコージとの一件以来、男に期待することはやめた。親友のカズコに自身がレズビアンであることをカミングアウトし、今ではレズの関係になっている。古き良き専業主婦として家を守る必要なくなり、彼女は自分らしく生きるための劇的な一歩を踏み出した彼女の厳しさは、誰の目にも印象的に映った。そして現在はバイクの修理工として、慎がよくバイクの修理で訪ねてくるガレージで働いている。

Risa wa Kōji to no ikken irai, otoko ni kitai suru koto wa yameta. Shin'yū no Kazuko ni jishin ga rezubian dearu koto wo kaminguauto shi, ima dewa rezu no kankei ni natte iru. Furuki yoki sengyō shufu to shite ie wo mamoru hitsuyō nakunari, kanojo wa jibunrashiku ikiru tame no gekitekina ippo wo fumidashita kanojo no kibishi-sa wa, dare no me ni mo inshō-teki ni utsutta. Soshite genzai wa baiku no shūrikō to shite, Shin ga yoku baiku no shūri de tazunete kuru garēji de hataraite iru.

I got sick and tired of being the only one who knew how to change the oil on a car, so I dumped Koji's bitch ass. Learn how to change a tire! We shouldn't rely on men to do this. Woman power!

私は1台の車のオイル交換の方法しか知らないことにうんざり疲れたから浩司のバカをふってやったわ。タイヤの交換方法ぐらい学べ！ 私たちはそれができる男に頼るべきではないわ。女子力を発揮させるのよ!

Watashi wa 1-dai no kuruma no oiru kōkan no hōhō shika shiranai koto ni unzari tsukareta kara Kōji no baka wo futte yatta wa. Taiya no kōkan hōhō gurai manabe! Watashitachi wa sore ga dekiru otoko ni tayorubeki dewa nai wa. Joshiryoku wo hakki saserunoyo!

CHAPTER 6 Words from the story used in phrases

Words from the story used in phrases

物語の単語を使って文を作る

リサの人生ストーリーのキーワードを使って例文を作ってみましょう。

Words from the story ストーリーのキーワード

Come Out
カミングアウト

Lesbian
レズビアン

Dramatic
劇的な

Tough As Nails
厳しい

Key Word_01

Come Out カミングアウト

Kaminguauto

His coming out wasn't a big surprise, as he didn't realize riding a pink bike would be such a dead giveaway.

彼はピンクのバイクに乗ることが秘密をばらすということになるとは気づかなかったため、カミングアウトすることはそんなに大きなサプライズにはならなかった。

kare wa pinku no baiku ni noru koto ga himitsu wo barasu toiu koto ni naru to wa kizukanakatta tame, kaminguauto surukoto wa sonna ni ookina sapuraizu ni wa naranakatta.

Key Word_02

Lesbian レズビアン
Rezubian

Not all lesbians dress like men, the same way not all men dress like men.

男が全員男らしい服を着ないのと同じで、レズビアンも全員男らしい服を着るわけではない。

Otoko ga zenin otokorashii fuku wo kinai no to onaji de rezubian mo zenin otoko rashii fuku wo kiru wake de wa nai.

Key Word_03

Dramatic 劇的な
Gekitekina

You need to make some dramatic changes in your life, otherwise you will end up dead!

自分の人生に劇的な変化を与えないと死んでしまうよ。

Jibun no jinsei ni gekitekina henka wo ataenai to shinde shimau yo.

Key Word_04

Tough As Nails 厳しい
Kibishii

The priest may have seemed tough as nails, but he had a soft spot for cute alter boys.

その牧師は厳しく見えたが教会の可愛い男の子たちには弱かった。

Sono bokushi wa kibishiku mieta ga kyoukai no kawai otokonoko tachi ni wa yowakatta.

CHAPTER 6 Lisa's Life Scenario 6
CD トラック 22

Lisa's Life Scenario 6
リサの人生シナリオ6「バイク修理屋」

テクニシャンのリサが慎にアドバイスする。

2: HAHAHA!
ハハハ
hahaha

4: You need to be creative Shin. Use your hands, oral sex, or in your case maybe a strap-on.
もうちょっと頭を使えよ、慎。手を使ったり、口を使ったり、お前の場合にはペニバンとかさ。
Mou chotto atama wo tsukae yo, Shin. Te wo tsukattari, kuchi wo tsukattari, omae no baai ni wa peniban toka sa.

6: Hell no!
絶対イヤ！
Zettai iya!

1: **Can you give me some advice? Emi said my dick was small.**

ちょっと聞いてほしいんだけど、エミが俺のは小さいって言ったんだよ。
Chotto kiite hoshinn dakedo, Emi ga ore no wa chisai tte ittanda yo.

3: **Don't laugh, this is serious! You don't have any dick at all, how do you even have sex?**

笑うなよ、こっちは超マジなんすよ！ ついてないクセにどうやってるんすか？
Warau na yo, kotchi wa cho maji nansuyo! Tsuitenai kuse ni dō yatterunsu ka?

5: **Strap-ons! Can I borrow one of yours?**

ペニスバンド！ それオレに貸してくれる？
Penisubando! Sore ore ni kashite kureru?

Important Phrases 重要なフレーズ

※ **Oral sex** オーラル セックス
口だけで性行為を行うこと。
Sex that does not involve penetration and is performed only with the mouth.

※ **Strap-on** ストラップ オン
ペニスバンドのこと。
An adult toy dildo that is strapped to the person's waist by a belt or harness.

Lisa-Things a feminist would say...
フェミニストのリサが言うフレーズ10

使うのに注意= ☠　注意= ☠☠　かなり危険= ☠☠☠

Phrase_01
Anything boys can do, girls can do better!
男の子ができることは、女の子はもっと上手くできる。
Otoko no ko ga dekiru koto wa onna no ko wa motto umaku dekiru.

Phrase_02 ☠
Guys like you, are why girls turn lesbian.
キミみたいな男がいるから女はレズになる。
Kimi mitai na okoto ga iru kara onna wa rezu ni naru.

Phrase_03 ☠☠☠
All I heard was, "Blah blah blah, I'm an asshole."
「なんとかかんとか、私はクソ野郎」しか聞こえなかった。
"nantoka kanatoka, watashi wa kuso yaro" shika kikoenakatta.

Phrase_04 ☠☠
Out of millions of sperm, you were the fastest?
何百万の精子の中で、キミが一番早かった？
Nannbyaku man no seishi no naka de, kimi ga ichiban hayakatta?

Phrase_05
There are enough advances in technology that we have little to no need for men.
テクノロジーが十分発展してるから、ほとんど男性の助けは必要ない。
Tekunoroji ga juubun kaihatsu shiteru kara hotondo no dansei no tasuke wa hitsuyou nai.

Phrase_06 ☠☠☠

The closest you will ever come to a woman is a **masturbation tube**.

一番お前が女性に近づけるのはオナホールだな。

1-chiban omae ga josei ni chikatsuke no wa onaho-ru dana.

Phrase_07

I'm impressed, you seemed to have exercised every muscle except for the one in your head.

感激したよ。あなたすごく筋トレしたのね、脳みそ以外は。

Kangeki shita yo. Anata sugoku kintore shita no ne, nomiso igai wa.

Phrase_08 ☠

I may not be able to stand and pee, but at least I wipe everytime.

立っておしっこはできないかもしれないが、せめて毎回ふく。

Tatte oshikko wa dekinai kamoshirenai ga, semete maikai fuku.

Phrase_09 ☠☠

I can grow a beard too, the difference is mine is below my waistline.

私はヒゲもはやせる、ただ違うのは、私のはウエストより下ってこと。

Watashi wa hige mo hayaseru, tada chigau no wa watshi no wa uesuto yori shitatte koto.

Phrase_10

I am not a vegetarian because I love animals. I am a vegetarian because I hate plants.

動物好きだから菜食主義ではない。植物が嫌いだから私は菜食主義。

Doubutsu sukidakara saishokushugi dewa nai. Shokubutsu ga kirai dakara watashi wa saishokushugi.

※Phrase_03: assholeは、stupid(バカ)やJerk(アホ)よりワンランク上の無礼な言葉。

※Phrase_04: 受精は、何百万の精子が受精競争して、たったひとつしか受精できない。生まれたのも確率的には低いのに、なぜこんなバカな人が生まれたんだろうという意味。

※Phrase_06: masturbationは、男性を幸せにできる魔法の筒のこと。ここでは男性器と同じものをつけないとダメだなという意味。

Lisa -Things a person would say to a feminist...
フェミニストのリサが言われたフレーズ10

使うのに注意= ☠   注意= ☠☠   かなり危険= ☠☠☠

Phrase_01 ☠
Do you experience penis envy?

ペ◯ス欲しいって、焼きもち抱いたことある？

Pe◯su hoshi tte yakimochi idaita koto aru?

Phrase_02 ☠☠☠
Cook, clean, raise babies is it really too much to ask?

料理、洗濯、子育てぐらい、いいでしょう？

Ryori, senntaku, kosodate gurai, ii deshou?

Phrase_03
I'd never hit a woman, but you're borderline enough to make an exception.

女を殴ったことはないが、お前の場合は例外になるギリギリのとこだな。

Onna wo nagutta koto wa naiga, omae no baai wa reigai ni naru girigiri no toko dana.

Phrase_04 ☠☠☠
You really should get back in the kitchen and shut the fuck up.※

黙ってキッチンに戻れ。

Damatte kicchin ni modore.

Phrase_05 ☠☠
Why don't you go do something productive like wash the dishes.

なんかやったらどうなんだ、皿洗いとか。

Nanka yattara dou nanda, sara aria toka.

Phrase_06 ☠☠☠

The smartest thing to come out of your mouth was a penis.

キミの口から出るので一番賢いのはペ◯スだね。

Kimi no kuchi kara deru node ichiban kashikoi no wa pe◯su da ne.

Phrase_07 ☠

Shhh... it's time for the men to talk.

シー、男が話す時間だ。

Shi, otoko ga hansu jikan da.

Phrase_08

Aww, it's so cute when you try to talk about things you don't understand.

あー、わからないことについて話そうとしてるときのキミってかわいいね。

Aa. wakaranai koto ni tsuite hanasou to shiteru toki no kimitte kawaii ne.

Phrase_09

Behind every successful man is his woman. Behind the fall of a successful man, is usually another woman.

成功しているすべての男性には女性がいる。失敗している男性には別の女性がいる。

Seikou shiteru subete no dansei ni wa josei ga iru. Shippai shiteru dansei ni wa betsu no josei ga iru.

Phrase_10 ☠

Do your bitchin' from the kitchen.

文句は台所からいえ。

Monku wa daidokoro kara ie

※Phrase_04:通常はPlease be quiet「静かにしてください」フレーズが基本。強く言うとShut up「黙って」となり、Fuckを入れるとShut the fuck up「黙れ！」と非常に強い命令口調になる。

※Phrase_06:相手の言うことは全部バカすぎて、その口は喋るためじゃなくてフェラチオだけに使ったほうがいいよという意味。

※Phrase_08:新しく覚えたことをまるでものすごく知ってるかのように他人に説明しようとしてる状況を見て、からかう時に使う。

CHAPTER 6 Helpful Words And Phrases GOOD & BAD

シナリオに関連する単語を使ったGOODとBADフレーズ
Helpful Words And Phrases
GOOD & BAD

Power tools 動力工具 Douryoku kougu

GOOD
There are amazing things you can build with power tools.
驚くほどすごいものが動力工具で組み立てられる。
Odoroku hodo sugoi mono ga dōryoku kōgu de kumitate rareru.

BAD
Some of the vibrators, are just as powerful as the power tools you own.
いくつかのバイブレーターは、お前が持っている動力工具ぐらいパワフルだ。
Ikutsuka no baibureda wa, omae ga motteiru douryoku gurai pawafuru da.

Oil change オイル交換 Oiru koukan

GOOD
Only lazy people don't know how to do an oil change on a car or bike.
車やバイクのオイル交換の仕方を知らないのは、怠け者だけだ。
Kuruma ya baiku no oirukoukan no shikata wo shiranai no wa namakemono dake da.

BAD
Do your own oil change, you lazy fuck!
車やバイクのオイル交換の仕方を知らないのは、怠け者だけだ。
Kuruma ya baiku no oiru koukan no shikata wo shiranai no wa namakemono dake da.

Tune up チューンナップ Chunnappu

GOOD
My bike runs like shit, I think it needs a tune up.
オレのバイクが全然だめだ、チューンナップがいるな。
Ore no baiku ga zenzen dame da, chunnappu ga iru na.

BAD
You ride your bike like a crazy fucking lunatic, no wonder it needs a tune up.
おまえのバイクの乗り方はメチャクチャだ、どうりでチューンナップがいるわけだ。
Omae no baiku no norikata wa mechakucha da, douri de chunnappu ga iruwake da.

Feminist フェミニスト Feminisuto

GOOD
Feminists don't think men are disposable, unless they are lesbians.
フェミニストにとって人は使い捨てだとは思わない、レズでなければ。
Feminisuto ni totte hito wa tsukaisuteda to wa omowanai, rezu denakereba.

BAD
It's not because you're a feminist that I dislike you, it's because you're a dike bitch.
オレがおまえを嫌いなのはフェミニストだからじゃない、おまえがレズ女だからだ！
Orega ga omae wo kirai na no wa feminisuto dakara jyanai, omae ga rezu onna dakara da!

CHAPTER 7

SHIN TANAKA
田中 慎

Shin's Life Story
田中 慎の人生

やんちゃ坊主だった慎も25歳になりました。道は外れていても気持ちは一途な彼はどんな人生を送っているか見てみましょう。

Shin's Life Story

Shin never studied for his English exams, and began to hate English and **westerners** all together. He later joined a pro-Japanese group and began committing small crimes and **petty theft**. In and out of jail, over the years his **street cred** led him to become the leader of a local biker gang. Yet he still remains good **buddies** with the only foreigner he likes, Billie Green, and is a member of Billie's Pilates and Yoga studio.

慎は英語の試験のために勉強をしたことがなく、英語と西洋人全部を嫌うようになった。やがて彼は日本びいきのグループに参加し、小さな犯罪やちょっとした盗みに手を染め始めていった。何年か刑務所を出入りする生活が続くと街の評判は彼をその地方の暴走族リーダーに仕立て上げることになった。しかし彼はたったひとりだけの外国人友だち、ビリー・グリーンと仲が良く、ビリーのピラティスとヨガクラブのメンバーでもある。

Shin wa eigo no shiken no tame ni benkyō wo shita koto ga naku, eigo to seiyō-jin zenbu wo kirau yō ni natta. Yagate kare wa Nihon-biki no gurūpu ni sankashi, chīsana hanzai ya chottoshita nusumi ni te wo some hajimete itta. Nan-nen ka keimusho wo deiri suru seikatsu ga tsudzuku to machi no hyōka wa kare wo sono chihō no bōzōzoku rīdā ni shitate ageru koto ni natta. Shikashi kare wa tatta hitori dake no gaikoku hito tomodachi, Biri Gurīn to naka ga yoku, Biri no piratisu to yoga kurabu no menbā demo aru.

Fuck authority! They can't even pull me over while I ride my bike up and down a busy street. If we are riding bicycles they may be able to stop us easily. So I say, always ride a motorcycle, like me!

くたばれ、政府の犬め！あいつらはバイクに乗っているオレを渋滞してる道でだって止められないんだ。もし自転車に乗っていれば、警察はオレたちを簡単に止めることができるかもね。だからオレみたいな奴は、いつもバイクに乗ってるんだよ！

Kutabare, seifuno inu me! Aitsu-ra wa baiku ni notte iru ore wo jūtaishi teru michi de datte tomerarenai nda. Moshi jitensha ni notte ireba, keisatsu wa ore-tachi wo kantan ni tomeru koto ga dekiru kamo ne. Dakara ore mitaina yatsu wa, itsumo baiku ni notterunda yo!

CHAPTER 7 Words from the story used in phrases

Words from the story used in phrases

物語の単語を使って文を作る

慎の人生ストーリーのキーワードを使って例文を作ってみましょう。

Words from the Story　ストーリーのキーワード

Westerners
西洋人

Petty Theft
ちょっとした盗み

Street Cred
街の評判(名声)

Buddies
友達

Key Word_01

Westerners 西洋人

Seiyoujin

Westerners are considered to have big noses and big cocks.

西洋人は鼻がでかくてアソコもでかいと考えられている。

Seiyoujin wa hana ga dekakute asoko mo dekai to kangaerarete iru.

Key Word_02

Petty Theft ちょっとした盗み
Chotto shita nusumi

I am a master thief. I would never get caught in a convenience store for petty theft.

オレは大泥棒だ。コンビニのちょっとした盗みでは絶対捕まらないね。

Ore wa oodorobo da. Konbini no chotto shita nusumi de wa zettai tsukamaranai ne.

Key Word_03

Street Cred 街の評判（名声）
Machi no hyoban(meisei)

He took on 10 guys with nothing but his fists and won. That's serious street cred.

彼はこぶしだけで10人の男を相手にして勝った。それはマジで街の評判になる。

Kare wa kobushi dake de 10-nin no otoko wo aite ni shite katta. Sore wa maji de machi no hyouban ni naru.

Key Word_04

Buddies 友達
Tomodachi

I wouldn't stab you in the back. We are buddies.

オレは裏切らないよ。オレたちは友達だ。

Ore wa uragiranai yo. Oretachi wa tomodachi da.

CHAPTER 7 Shin's Life Scenario 7 | CD トラック 26

1: Get back here, you little shit!
戻ってこい、小僧!
Modotte koi kozou!

3: When I catch you, you're dead Shin! You hear me, punk?
お前を捕まえたら殺すからな!
わかってんのか、コラ!
Omae tsukamaetara korosu kara na! Wakatten no ka kora!

Shin's Life Scenario 7
慎の人生シナリオ7「ハイウェイにて」

慎はエリミネーターから逃げる。

2: I'll pay you back next week, I promise!

来週お金払うから、約束する!
Raishu okane harau kara, yakusoku suru!

4: If you catch me!

捕まえれたらね!
Tsukamaetara ne!

Important Phrases　重要なフレーズ

※ **Little shit**　リトル シット
相手を見下して侮辱した呼ぶときに使う。
A way to insult someone and make them feel small.

※ **Punk**　パンク
権力やほか誰にも敬意を払わない不良のこと。
A delinquent or person who does not respect authority.

CHAPTER 7 Things to say to a delinquent Japanese punk...

CD トラック 27

Shin - Things to say to a delinquent Japanese punk...
ヤンキーの慎が言われた屈辱フレーズ10

使うのに注意＝ ☠　注意＝ ☠☠　かなり危険＝ ☠☠☠

Phrase_01
You are proof that evolution can go in reverse.
進化過程が逆にもなるってことをあなたは証明したね。
Shinka katei ga gyaku ni monaru tte koto wo anata wa shomei shita ne.

Phrase_02
Are you always an idiot, or just when I'm around.
あなたはいつもマヌケなの？ それとも私がいるときだけ？
Anata itsumo manuke na no? Sore tomo watashi ga iru toki dake?

Phrase_03
You drive so bad, you prefer three left turns to one right turn.
あんたって運転下手、1回右に曲がるんじゃなくて3回左に曲がるんだね。
Anta tte unten heta, 1-kai migi ni magarun janakute 3-kai hidari ni magarun da ne.

Phrase_04
You can't be a badass, if your mom still makes your bento.
母ちゃんに弁当をまだ作ってもらってるんだったら、ダッセーな。
Kāchan ni bentō wo mada tsukutte moratteru n dattara, dasse na.

Phrase_05
That hairstyle went out of style several decades ago.
キミの髪型は、数10年前に流行ったよね。
Kimi no kamigata wa, sū 10-nen mae ni hayatta yo ne.

Phrase_06
Nice outfit, I wasn't aware the circus was in town.

いい服だね、サーカスが町にきてるって知らなかったよ。

Ii fuku da ne, sakasu ga machi ni kiteru tte shiranakatta yo.

Phrase_07
※Don't steal. That's the government's job.

盗みはやるなよ、それは政府のやる仕事だから。

Nusumi wa yaru nayo, sore wa seifu no yaru shigoto dakara.

Phrase_08
Say no to drugs.

薬物反対。

Yakubutsu hantai.

Phrase_09
Stay in school, fool!

バカ、学校サボるな！

Baka, gakkou saboru na!

Phrase_10
You're so stupid, it takes you an hour to cook minute rice.※

バカだな、あんたならインスタントライスを作るのに1時間かかるよ。

Baka da na, anata nara insutantoraisu tsukuru no ni 1-jikan kakaru yo.

※Phrase_04: badassは、直訳すると悪い意味にとらえがちですが、恰好のいい人に使うホメ言葉です。

※Phrase_07: 海外では、国民が国に払うお金（税金）が多すぎることを政府が国民からお金を盗んでるという例えを使って表現します。自分がされて嫌なことを人にするのかという意味で盗みをしようとしてる人を止める時に使う言葉。

※Phrase_10: minute riceつまりインスタント米のこと。レンジでチンするだけなのに、何分でできあがるかよく読んでないか読めないぐらいアホという表現。

CHAPTER 7　Things to say to insult foreigners...　CD トラック 28

Shin -Things to say to insult foreigners...
ヤンキーの慎が外国人を挑発したフレーズ10

使うのに注意= ☠　注意= ☠☠　かなり危険= ☠☠☠

Phrase_01
How many seasons do you have in your country?
あなたの国では季節はいくつあるの？
Anata no kuni de wa kisetsu wa ikutsu aru no?

Phrase_02
Wow, you can use chopsticks so well!
わぉ! お箸の使い方上手ね!
Wao! Ohashi no tsukai kata jozu ne!

Phrase_03 ☠
**Japanese don't smell bad,
why do you foreigners stink?**
日本人はくさくないけど、なんで外国人ってにおうの？
Nihonjin wa kusakunai kedo, nande gaikokujintte niou no?

Phrase_04
※
You mean, you are not from America?
あなたってアメリカ出身じゃないの？
Anata tte amerika shushinn jyanai no?

Phrase_05 ☠☠☠
※
What's up my nigga?
調子はどうだい、兄弟？（ニガー）
Chōshi wa dō dai, kyōdai?

118　DARK HORIZON CHAPTER-07

Phrase_06 ☠

I can't believe you guys ban hentai manga featuring children. Don't you love children?

児童の変態漫画禁止令なんて信じられない。子供好きじゃないの？

Jido no hentai manga kinshirei nante shinjirarenai, kodomo sukijyanai no?

Phrase_07 ☠☠☠

Why are you all so fat?

なんでみんなデブなの？

Nande mina debu na no?

Phrase_08 ☠

You have a fucking small head.

お前の顔、マジ小さいね。

Omae no kao maji chiisai ne.

Phrase_09 ☠☠

You have a big fucking nose.

お前の鼻はマジでかい。

Omae no hana wa maji dekai.

Phrase_10 ☠☠☠

How big is your penis?

お前のペ○スどのぐらいの大きさ？

Omae no pe○su dono gurai no ookisa?

※Chapter_04: 日本人がよく勘違いしがちなのは、外国人＝アメリカ人というイメージが多いこと。そのため、これを聞いたカナダ人やイギリス人などがよく怒ります。You mean〜は「つまり〜」という意味。再び繰り返して聞く場合に使う強調文。

※Phrase_05: niggaは、brotherという意味合いで黒人同士友人の場合に使いますが、日本人がいきなり使うと大変危険だ。

※Chapter_06: hentai mangaは、英語でも通じるほど、一般的な単語。

※Phrase_07〜10: 日本人がいいイメージだと思って言う「顔が小さい」や「鼻が高い」は、外国人には決してホメ言葉ではありません。意味のないただの不快な会話になります。これを言われた外国人は、イメージだけで会話する日本人を視野が狭いと感じるだろう。(本人経験談)

CHAPTER 7 Helpful Words And Phrases GOOD & BAD

シナリオに関連する単語を使ったGOODとBADフレーズ

Helpful Words And Phrases
GOOD & BAD

Pigs おまわり Omawari

GOOD
Quick, we need to get out of here now before the pigs show up!
急げ、おまわりがくる前にここから逃げるんだ！
Isoge, omawari ga kuru mae ni koko kara nigerun da!

BAD
Flush the drugs before the pigs arrive, or we are all going to get busted!
おまわりがくる前にヤクを全部トイレに流せ、でないとオレたちみんなつかまっちまうぞ。
Omawari ga kuru mae ni yaku wo zenbu toire ni nagase, denai to oretachi minna tsukamacchimauzo!

Screwed しくじった Shigujitta

GOOD
I can't help but think when your mom finds out, we are both screwed.
オレたちがしくじったことを知ったときのお前のお袋さんのことを考えられずにはいられない。
Oretachi ga shigujitta koto wo shitta toki no omae no ofukurosan no koto wo kangaerarezu ni wa irarenai.

BAD
I shit my pants on the train and arrived late, so my interview was screwed.
電車の中で漏らして着くのが遅れてしまい、面接をしくじった。
Densha no naka de morashite tsuku no ga okurete shimai, mensetsu wo shikujitta.

Rebel 裏切り者／反抗 Uragirimono / Hanko

GOOD
The consequences don't matter, she is a rebel and doesn't care.
結果は関係なく、彼女は裏切り者だから知ったことじゃない。
Kekka wa kankei naku, kanojo wa uragirimono dakara shittakotoja nai.

BAD
The first time a child rebels against your authority, slap them so hard their head bounces off the floor.
初めて子どもがあなたの権力に反抗するとき、彼らの頭が床で跳ね返るほど思いっきり引っぱたく。
Hajimete kodomo ga anata no kenryoku ni hankō suru toki, karera no atama ga yuka de hanekaeru hodo omoikkiri hippataku.

Ghetto スラム街 Suramugai

GOOD
Growing up in ghetto is hard, I don't care about the people still stuck there!
スラム街で育つのはきつい、オレはいまだにそこにとどまっている人間は気にしない。
Suramugai de sodatsu no wa kitsui, ore wa imadani soko ni todomatte iru ningen wa kinishinai.

BAD
Your apartment is ghetto as hell; I wouldn't sleep there if you paid me.
てめえのアパートはあの世みたいなスラム街だ、もし金をもらってもあそこには寝たりしないぜ。
Temē no apāto wa anoyo mitaina suramugai da, moshi kane wo moratte mo asoko ni wa netari shinai ze.

CHAPTER 8

KAZUKO SATO
佐藤 カズコ

Kazuko's Life Story
佐藤 カズコの人生

教師だった佐藤先生は、たくさんのストレスを抱えた結果、
意外な道を見つけました。どんな人生を送っているか見てみましょう。

Kazuko's Life Story

The stress of teaching caused her to gain weight and she decided to quit and pursue her real **passion**: wrestling. Winning multiple championships, she was eventually forced her to **retire** due to a sports related injury. After Lisa's coming out, the two moved in together and Kazuko used her **winnings** to open a small cafe. Not one to let an opportunity slip her by, the cafe has become a **popular** front for local Yakuza, to launder their money and push product from the Chinese triads.

教師でいることのストレスは、彼女の体重を増大させ、彼女は教師を辞めて本当の情熱に従う事を決意した……それはレスリングだった。いくつもの試合でチャンピオンとして優勝を飾ったが、競技上のケガから引退を余儀なくされた。リサのレズビアンのカミングアウトの後、二人は一緒に住み始め、カズコはファイトマネーを使って小さなカフェを開いた。やがてそのカフェはヤクザが資金運用の為に中国の貿易商からの商品を扱う恰好の隠し場所として利用することで繁盛をしていった。

Kyōshi de iru koto no sutoresu wa kanojo no taijū wo zōdai sa se, kanojo wa kyōshi wo yamete hontō no jōnetsu ni shitagau koto wo ketsui shita…… soreha resuringu datta. Ikutsu mo no shiai de chanpion to shite yūshō wo kazattaga, kyōgi-jō no kega kara intai wo yoginaku sa reta. Risa no rezubian no kaminguauto no ato, futari wa issho ni sumi hajime, Kazuko wa faitomanē wo tsukatte chīsana kafe wo hiraita. Yagate sono kafe wa yakuza ga shikin un'yō no tame ni Chūgoku no bōeki-shō kara no shōhin wo atsukau kakkō no kakushibasho to shite riyō suru koto de hanjō wo shite itta.

There are still many sports dominated by men, but all we need is strong girls like me to show them that gender makes no difference. I only wish I could grow a beard, I already know I have bigger balls than most men!

まだまだたくさんのスポーツが男に支配されているけど、私たち全員に必要なのは、性別に差は無いってことを私のような強い女が証明するべきなんだ。私はすでに男たちよりデカイ金玉を持っているのがわかっているから、せめてヒゲだけでも伸ばせればって願っているよ!

Madamada takusan no supōtsu ga otoko ni shihai sarete irukedo, watashitachi zen'in ni hitsuyōna no wa, seibetsu ni sa wa nai tte koto wo watashi no yōna tsuyoi on'na ga shōmei surubeki nanda. Watashi wa sudeni otoko-tachi yori dekai kintama wo motte iru no ga wakatte irukara, semete hige dake demo nobasereba tte negatte iru yo!

CHAPTER 8 Words from the story used in phrases

Words from the story used in phrases

物語の単語を使って文を作る

カズコの人生ストーリーのキーワードを使って例文を作ってみましょう。

Words from the story　ストーリーのキーワード

Passion
情熱

Retire
引退

Winnings
戦利品

Popular
人気

Key Word_01

Passion 情熱

Jyounetsu

I have a passion for large knives and ear wax.

私は耳クソと大きなナイフに情熱を持っている。

Watashi wa mimi kuso to ookina naifu ni jyonetsu wo motteiru.

Key Word_02

Retire 引退
Intai

**That fat bastard will never retire.
We need to find a way to kill him off.**

あのデブ野郎は絶対辞めないだろう。私たちは彼をくたばらせる方法を見つける必要がある。

Ano debu yaro wa zettai yamenai darou. watashitachi wa kare wo kudabaraseru hou hou wo mitsukeru hitsuyou ga aru.

Key Word_03

Winnings 戦利品
Senrihin

In poker, the only way to collect real winnings is to cheat.

ポーカーで勝つたったひとつの方法は、だますことである。

Pōkā de katsu tatta hitotsu no hōhō wa, damasu koto dearu.

Key Word_04

Popular 人気
Ninki

**Just because you are popular,
doesn't mean you can just shit on everyone else.**

人気があるということだけで皆を見下せるということではない。

Ninki ga aru to iu koto dake de mina wo mikudaseru to iu koto dewa nai.

CHAPTER 8 Kazuko's Life Scenario 8 — CD トラック 30

1: Yeah! Destroy him! Body slam! Headlock!

おっしゃー！やったれ！叩き潰せ！ヘッドロックかませ！
Osha! Yattare! Tatakitsubuse! Heddorokku kamase!

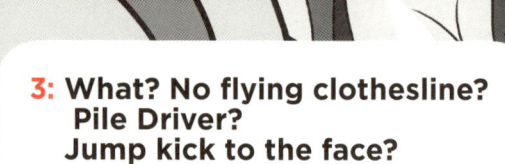

3: What? No flying clothesline? Pile Driver? Jump kick to the face?

なに？ フライング・ラリアットもダメ？ パイルドライバーもダメ？ 顔蹴りも？
Nani? Furaingu rariatto mo dame? Pairudoraiba mo dame? Kao geri mo?

5: Ohhh...

はぁ〜
Haa

Kazuko's Life Scenario 8
カズコの人生シナリオ8「相撲観戦」

カズコは生まれて初めて相撲を見に行った。

2: I don't think they are allowed to do that in this sport.

このスポーツでそれをやっちゃいけないと思うよ。
Kono supotsu de sore wo yaccha ikenai to omou yo!

4: No, No and No. This is traditional Japanese wrestling!

ダメ、ダメ、それもダメ。
これは日本の伝統的な国技なのよ。
Damedashi, damedashi, sore mo dame.
Kore wa nihon no
dentouteki na kougi nanoyo.

Important Phrases 重要なフレーズ

※Body Slam　ボディ スラム
手の体を地面に叩きつけるプロレスの技のこと。
When someone is picked up in a fight and thrown to the ground on their back.

※ Flying Clothesline　フライング クローズライン
プロレスなどでリングのコーナーに上りジャンプし相手に突っ込む技のこと。
When a wrestler jumps off the top ropes and hits their opponent in the face.

※ Pile Driver　パイル ドライバー
相手を逆さまの状態で持ち上げて太ももで挟み地面に頭から叩きつける技のこと。
When a someone is picked up by their feet, their head between the legs of their opponent, and dropped headfirst to the ground.

Kazuko -Things to say to a female wrestler...

女子プロレスラー、カズコが言われたフレーズ10

使うのに注意= ☠ 注意= ☠☠ かなり危険= ☠☠☠

Phrase_01 ☠

You are fat.

デブ。
Debu.

Phrase_02 ☠

I thought female wrestlers were supposed to be sexy too.

女子プロレスラーはみんなセクシーさもあるハズと思っていたよ。
Joshi puroresurā wa min'na sekushī-sa mo aru hazu to omotte ita yo.

Phrase_03

If you want to make the big bucks: you are going to need to involve some mud.

大金をつかみたいなら、ドサまわりして泥んこプロレスをする覚悟も必要だ。
Taikin wo tsukamitainara, dosamawari shite doronko puroresu wo suru kakugo mo hitsuyōda.

Phrase_04 ☠☠☠

What size bra do you wear?

ブラのサイズは？
Bura no saizu wa?

Phrase_05

Have you considered getting into sumo?

相撲界に入ることは考えなかったの？
Sumokai ni hairu koto wa kangenakatta no?

Phrase_06

Are you thinking what I'm thinking? No, because I'm not thinking about cake.

私と同じこと考えてる？ ちがうよ(あなたと同じように)、だってケーキのことなんて考えてないし。

Watashi to onaji koto kangaeteru? Chigauyo, date keki no koto nante kangaetenai shi.

Phrase_07 ☠☠☠

When was the last time you saw your whole body in the mirror?

最後に全身を鏡で見たのいつ？

Siago ni zenshi wo kagami de mita no itsu?

Phrase_08 ☠☠☠
※
Where is your neck?

首はどこ？(太り過ぎのため首がうまっている)

Kubi wa doko?

Phrase_09 ☠☠☠

Are you collecting chins※?

お前、二重あごだな！

Omae nijuu ago dana!

Phrase_10
※
You fake it better than my last girlfriend.

キミうまく芝居がかってるね、前の彼女よりうまいよ。

Kimi umaku shibaigakatteru ne, mae no kanojo yori umai yo.

※Phrase_03: involve some mudつまり泥んこプロレスは、セクシーなビキニを着て戦う賞金額が高い試合。

※Phrase_05: getting intoは、スポーツや趣味にハマったときに使う表現。

※Phrase_08、09: 太り過ぎて首が脂肪で埋まっているという意味。また太っている人はあごが複数あるように見えるので、複数形chinsとなる。

※Phrase_10: セックスするときに彼女が気持ちよさそうに演じているふりに対してかけているフレーズ。レスリングもすべて演技なので、レスリングが芝居がかり過ぎていることを意味する。

Kazuko -Things to say as a wrestler/strong person (to a skinny/weak person)...
女子プロレスラー、カズコが使うフレーズ10

使うのに注意=☠ 注意=☠☠ かなり危険=☠☠☠

Phrase_01 ☠☠☠
I'll fucking squash you!

ぶっ潰してやる！

Butsubushite yaru!

Phrase_02 ☠☠☠
Take another step, and I'll end you.

もう一歩踏み出したら、お前はおわりだ。

Mou ippou fumidashitara, omae wa owari da.

Phrase_03 ☠☠☠
You're so skinny your nipples touch.

お前はやせすぎて両方の乳首がくっついちゃってるぞ。

Omae wa yasesugite ryouhou no chikubi ga kuttsuichatteru zo.

Phrase_04
I'd hug you, but I am afraid I will snap you in two.

ハグしたいけど、キミをまっぷたつに折っちゃうんじゃないかと心配だ。

Hagu shitaikedo, kimi wo mapputatsu ni otchaun janai ka to shinpai da.

Phrase_05 ☠☠☠
You look like you're getting ready for a trip to some starving nation.

食べものがない国にでも旅行に行くみたいだね。(ガリガリだから)

Tabemono ga nai kuni ni demo ryokou ni iku mitai da ne.

Phrase_06 ☠☠

If you ate a meatball, you would look like you were pregnant.

ミートボール食べたら、妊娠しているように見えるよ。

Mitoboru tabetara, ninshin shiteru you ni mieru yo.

Phrase_07 ☠

Just being skinny won't make you look like a supermodel. You have to actually look good.

たんに細いからといってモデルには見えることはない。外見が良くなきゃ。

Tan'ni hosoikara to itte moderu ni wa mieru koto wa nai. Gaiken ga yokunakya.

Phrase_08 ☠☠☠

You have the body of a prepubescent girl.

思春期直前の女の子みたいな体してるね。

Shishunki chokuzen no onna no ko mitai na karada shiterune.

Phrase_09

You are so skinny, you need to run around the shower to get wet.

ガリガリだから濡らすためにシャワーの周りを駆けまわらなきゃダメだね。

Garigari dakara nurasutameni shawa no mawari wo kakemawaranakya dame dane.

Phrase_10

I don't have a beer gut, I have a protective covering for my rock-hard abs.

ビール腹ではないが、オレの固い腹筋を保護するカバーはしてるぜ。

Biru bara de wa nai ga, ore no katai fukkin wo hogo suru kaba wa shiteruze.

※Phrase_06: 女性は細いので、ミートボールを食べたらお腹が出るという意味。ミートボールを使ったフレーズはアメリカでよく使われる。

※Phrase_08: オッパイが小さい女性に対して、思春期前の女子＝オッパイが小さいことにかけて使う失礼な表現。

※Phrase_09: シャワーヘッドの直径にも満たないほど、痩せているという意味。

※Phrase_10: お腹が出ている人が強がりで言うセリフ。rock hard absは、石みたいに固いお腹の筋肉のこと。

CHAPTER 8 — Helpful Words And Phrases GOOD & BAD

シナリオに関連する単語を使ったGOODとBADフレーズ

Helpful Words And Phrases
GOOD & BAD

Titties オッパイ Oppai

GOOD
It's not the size of the titties that matters, it's the shape!
オッパイは大きさじゃない、形が大事なんだ！
Oppai wa ookisa jyanai, katachi ga daiji nan da!

BAD
Her titties are so perfect, I want to breast fed.
彼女のオッパイは、完璧すぎて乳を飲みたいぐらいだ。
Kanojo no oppai wa kanpeki sugite chichi wo nomitai gurai da.

Thick 太い Futoi

GOOD
After eating nothing but ice cream for the past two months she looked thick.
この2カ月間アイスクリームしか食べなかったから、彼女太ったみたいだ。
Kono 2-kagetsukan aisusukurimu shika tabenakatta kara, kanojo futotta mitai da.

BAD
That hot mom pushing the stroller has a thick ass.
ベビーカーを押して歩くあのイケてるママは、でかいケツをしている。
Beibika wo oshite aruku, ano iketeru mama wa, dekai ketsu wo shiteiru.

Traditional 伝統 Dentou

GOOD
The tea ceremony is a traditional art going back hundreds of years.
茶道は数百年前から続く伝統芸術だ。
Sado wa suuhyakunen mae kara tsutsuku, dentou geijutsu da.

BAD
I find history and traditional arts boring, lets get fucked up and do some blow.
歴史とか伝統なんてつまんねえ、さっさとヤクでもやろうぜ。
Rekishi toka dentou nante tsumanne, sassa to yaku demo yarou ze.

Wrestle 格闘 Kakutou

GOOD
I will pay you money to wrestle that homeless man.
もしお前がホームレスの男と格闘するぐらいなら金をやる。
Moshi omae ga homuresu no otoko to kakutou suru nara, kane wo yaru.

BAD
I would wrestle you, but your 100kg out of my weight class fatty.
お前と格闘するにしても、お前は100キロもオレより太ってるんだぞ。
Omae to kakutou suru ni shitemo, omae wa 100-kiro mo ore yori futotterun da zo!

9

CHAPTER

BILLIE GREEN
ビリー・グリーン

CHAPTER 9 Billie's Life Story
CD トラック 33

Billie's Life Story
ビリー・グリーンの人生

アンの弟も23歳になり、カナダから日本に来日後、人生に大きな変化が待ち受けていた。どんな人になっているか見てみましょう。

Billie's Life Story

When Billie first came to Japan he immediately fell in love with the feminine visual kei bands, which led him to experiment with his own masculinity. After becoming very active in the cosplay scene he decided he felt more comfortable dressing as a woman. After a little nip and tuck he was reborn as "Billie Jean." He opened his own fitness studio to keep himself in shape and leave the door open to see his secret man crush Shin Tanaka.

ビリーは来日してすぐにフェミニンなビジュアル系バンドにハマり、その経験が彼にとっての男らしさに疑問を持つ引き金となった。精力的にコスプレ活動をする中で彼は女装をすることに心地よさを感じることに気づき、ちょっとした美容整形を経て「ビリージーン」として生まれ変わった。自分自身のボディラインのキープのためと、密かに想っている男、田中慎と会う口実のためにフィットネスクラブを始めた。

Biri wa rainichi shite sugu ni femininna bijuarukeibando ni hamari, sono keiken ga kare ni totte no otokorashi-sa ni gimon wo motsu hikigane to natta. Seiryoku-teki ni kosupure katsudō wo suru naka de kare wa josō wo suru koto ni kokochiyo-sa wo kanjiru koto ni kidzuki, chottoshita biyō seikei wo hete 'Birījīn' toshite umarekawatta. Jibunjishin'no bodi rain no kīpu no tame to, hisoka ni omotte iru otoko, Tanaka Shin to au kōjitsu no tame ni fittonesukurabu wo hajimeta.

I hang out in Shinjuku 2-chome sometimes, if I am looking for a quick one-night stand. Being a bi-sexual means the other half of the population is fair game! I like those odds!

たまに新宿2丁目で、ひと晩だけの相手を探すときに遊んでいるわ。バイセクシャルでいるってことは人口の半分と楽しんじゃってもいいってことよ。私はこの確率性の高さがたまんないの!

Tamani Shinjuku 2-chōme de, hitoban dake no aite wo sagasu toki ni asonde iru wa. Baisekusharu de iru tte koto wa jinkō no hanbun to tanoshin jatte mo ītte koto yo. Watashi wa kono kakuritsusei no takasa ga taman'naino!

CHAPTER 9 Words from the story used in phrases

Words from the story used in phrases

物語の単語を使って文を作る

ビリーの人生ストーリーのキーワードを使って例文を作ってみましょう。

Words from the story　ストーリーのキーワード

Feminine
女性的、フェミニンな

Masculinity
男らしさ

Reborn
生まれ変わった

Man Crush
好きな男性（ゲイ用語）

Key Word_01

Feminine 女性的、フェミニンな

Joseiteki, Femininna

I thought you were gay because your way of speaking is very feminine.

話し方が女性っぽいので私はあなたがゲイだと思った。

Hanashikata ga joseippoi no de watashi wa anata ga gei da to omotta.

Key Word_02

Masculinity 男らしさ
Otokorashisa

No need to show off your masculinity. I can see your ball sack just fine through your tight shorts.

あなたの玉袋が短パンからよく見えるから、その男らしさを見せつける必要はない。

Anata no kintama bukuro ga tanpan kara yoku mieru kara otoko rashisa wo misetsukeru hitsuyou wa nai.

Key Word_03

Reborn 生まれ変わった
Umare kawatta

If you do bad deeds now, you may be reborn as a cockroach.

もしこの世で悪いことをしたら、ゴキブリになって生まれ変わるかもしれません。

Moshi kono yo de warui koto wo shitara, gokiburi ni natte umare kawaru kamoshiremasen.

Key Word_04

Man Crush 好きな男性（ゲイ用語）
Suki na dansei

It's not ok to follow your man-crush into the bathroom stall.

好きな男性をトイレまで追いかけるのはよくない。

Sukina dansei wo toire made oikakeru no wa yokunai.

CHAPTER 9 Billie's Life Scenario 9

CD トラック **34**

2: It's important to open your chakras for optimal flow of energy.

チャクラからね、精神的なね、
エネルギーをね、循環させるためにはね、
大事なポーズよ。
Chakura wa ne, seishinteki na ne,
enerugi wo ne, junkan saseru tameniwane,
daiji na pozu yo.

4: Nonsense, it's good for your spiritual energy!

なに言ってんのよ。精神的な
エネルギーにとてもいいのよ。
Nani itten no yo. Seishin-tekina
enerugī ni totemo ī no yo.

6: No pain, no gain. Now spread 'em!

痛みなくして得るものはないわ。
開脚よ！
Itami nakushite erumono wa nai wa.
Kaikyaku yo!

Billie's Life Scenario 9
ビリーの人生シナリオ9「フィットネススタジオ」

ビリーは一生懸命ヨガのポーズを教える。

1: I don't know if I feel comfortable doing that pose.

そのポーズやるのはちょっと……。
Sono pozu yaru no wa chotto…

3: Yes, but I feel exposed.

うん、でもちょっと恥ずかしいわ。
Un, demo chotto hazukashii wa.

5: It looks painful!

痛そうに見える！
Itasou ni mieru!

Important Phrases 重要なフレーズ

※Chakras　チャクラ
ヨガではチャクラは、体の精神的なエネルギーポイントになる。
Mystical points of energy on your body.

※Spread 'em　スプレッドエム
手、足、お尻など体の一部を広げる動作。
Used when telling someone to open their arms, legs, or butt-cheeks.

CHAPTER 9 Things to say to a gay man in drag...

CD トラック **35**

Billie -Things to say to a gay man in drag...
ゲイのビリーが言われたフレーズ10

使うのに注意= ☠　注意= ☠☠　かなり危険= ☠☠☠

Phrase_01 ☠☠
You would like to swing both ways, but the chain broke somewhere and now you're stuck.

両天秤にかけたいと思っていても、なにか壊れて行き詰まってしまった。
Ryōtenbin ni kaketai to omotte ite mo, nanika kowarete ikidzumatte shimatta.

Phrase_02 ☠☠☠
I've seen transvestites who look more feminine than you.

お前より可愛いオカマを見たことがあるぜ。
Omae yori kawai okama wo mita koto ga aru ze.

Phrase_03
Does everything you make have to be fucking pink?

なんでお前はすべてピンクに作るんだい？
Nande omae wa subete pinku ni tsukurundai?

Phrase_04
When you speak it sounds like you have a permanent wedgie.

パンツを上げてるぐらいで女の声を出してんじゃねよ。
Pantsu wo ageteru gurai de onna no koe wo dashiterun jyane yo.

Phrase_05 ☠☠☠
You look worse than one of those ladyboys in Thailand.

お前はタイにいるオカマより気持ち悪いな。
Omae wa tai niiru okama yori kimochi warui na.

Phrase_06 💀💀💀
At first I thought you were crazy but now I can plainly see your nuts.※

最初はいい女だと思ったけど、よく見たら金玉ついてんのかよ!?

Saisho wa ii onna da to omotta kedo, yoku mitara kintama tsuiten no kayo!?

Phrase_07 💀💀💀
Which side of the onsen do you go in?

温泉に行ったときは、どっちに入るの？

Onsen ni itta toki wa docchi ni hairu no?

Phrase_08
Put on more foundation to cover that stubble.

青ひげを隠すようにもっとファンデーションを塗れよ。

Aohige wo kakusuyou ni, motto fandeshon wo nureyo.

Phrase_09 💀💀💀
How many guys can participate in a gang bang※ before it's gay?

ゲイの前は乱交パーティで何人の男と関係できた？

Gei no mae wa rankō pāti de nannin no otoko to kankei dekita?

Phrase_10 💀💀💀
So, which half is new?

どっからが女？どっからが男？

Dokkara ga onna? Dokkara ga otoko?

※Phrase_02、05: transvestitesは、女装した男や男装した女を指す。ladyboysは、女装した男でゲイの人を言う。

※Phrase_04: permanent wedgieとは、いたずらで勝手に相手のパンツを持ち上げてお尻に食い込ませること。

※Phrase_06: ここで言うnutsは、金玉のこと。ほかballsとも言う。

※Phrase_09: gang bangは、グループセックス、つまり乱交パーティを意味する。男ばっかりの乱交パーティはゲイパーティで、そういう風になるまでに何人の男は乱交パーティーに参加していいかという質問。

Billie -Things to say as a gay man in drag...
ゲイのビリーが言うフレーズ10

使うのに注意=☠   注意=☠☠   かなり危険=☠☠☠

Phrase_01 ☠☠☠
You may find booty sex distasteful, but I find it simply fabulous!

あなたはまだアナルのよさを知らないのね。
Anata ha mada anaru no yosa wo shiranai no ne.

Phrase_02
Is that banana in your pocket or are you just happy to see me?

もっこりしてるけど、どんだけ私に会いたかったの？
Mokkoroshi shiteru kedo, dondake watashi ni aitakatta no?

Phrase_03 ☠
You can kiss my ass, but you have to wait in line.

おととい、きてちょーだい。
Ototoi kite chodai.

Phrase_04
Who knows what a man wants better than a man?

男より男の欲しいことを知ってる奴なんていないわ。
Otoko yori otoko no hoshiikoto wo shitteru yatsu nantei naiwa.

Phrase_05
Sex with men is fun.

男とセックスするのは楽しいわよ。
Otoko to sekkusu suru no wa tanoshi wayo.

Phrase_06

I only say I'm gay when ugly girls and hot guys hit on me.

私はイケメンとブスと会ったときにしかカミングアウトしないわ。

Atashi ha ikemen to busu to atta toki ni shika kaminguauto shinai wa.

Phrase_07

These panties have no cup support

女性物下着をはくと、はみ出しちゃうのよ。

Josei mono shitagi wo haku to hami dashichau no yo.

Phrase_08 ☠☠

I'm shaved nose to toes!

私は全身脱毛してるわよ。

Watashi wa zenshin datsumo shiteruwayo.

Phrase_09

I don't think KY means the same thing in Japan as it does where I am from.

KYって日本では空気読めない奴を言うけど、私の国ではローションのことよ。

KY tte nihon de wa kuuki yomenai yatsu wo iukedo, watashi no kuni de wa roshon no koto yo.

Phrase_10 ☠☠☠

I will put a boot up your ass... or a heel if it's the weekend.

平日にそんなこと言ったら殺すところだけど、週末なら……いいわよ、セックス。

Heijitsu ni sonna koto ittara korosu tokoro dakedo, shumatsu nara… ii wayo, sekusu.

※Phrase_03: kiss my assは、直訳するとお尻にキスするですが、あり得ないことなので、ふざけるなという意味を持つ。

※Phrase_06: hit onは、ナンパを意味する。

※Phrase_10: put a boot up your ass とは、お尻をブーツで蹴飛ばす、つまり絶対にダメということを意味する。

CHAPTER 9 Helpful Words And Phrases GOOD & BAD

シナリオに関連する単語を使ったGOODとBADフレーズ

Helpful Words And Phrases
GOOD & BAD

Fit 元気 Genki

GOOD
A girl must not only be intelligent, she must be fit and able to cook!
女は頭がいいだけじゃなく、元気で料理ができなくちゃ！
Onna wa atama ga ii dake jyanakute, genki de ryouri ga deki nakucha!

BAD
Sexercise is a good way to stay fit.
セクササイズは元気でいるためのいい方法だ。
Sekusasaize wa genki de iru tame no ii houhou da.

Wedgie パンツの食い込み Pantsu no kuikomi

GOOD
I got a wedgie riding on my bike all day.
オレはバイクに乗っている間1日中パンツを食い込ませていた。
Ore wa baiku ni notteru aida ichinichi jyuu pantsu wo kuikomasete ita.

BAD
A wedgie on a hot summer day is nothing but a hot sticky mess when you take your pants off.
暑い夏の日のパンツの食い込みは、脱ぐとき暑さでべったりついていてひどいもんだ。
Atsui natsu no hi no pantsu no kuikomi wa, nugu toki atsusa de bettari tsuite ite hidoi monda.

Sweaty 汗をかく Ase wo kaku

GOOD
I get hot and sweaty just thinking about you.
キミのことを考えただけで、熱くなり汗をかく。
Kimi no koto wo kangaeta dake de, atsukunari ase wo kaku.

BAD
It must be 40 degrees outside, even my balls are sweaty.
外はきっと40度あるだろう、オレの玉さえ汗をかいている。
Soto wa kitto 40-do arudarou, ore no tama sae ase wo kaiteiru.

Camel Toe アソコの食い込み Asoko no kuikomi

GOOD
When Judy wears tight pants, my eyes are drawn to her camel toe.
ジュディがぴっちりしたパンツを履いているときは、オレの視線は彼女のアソコの食い込みに釘づけになった。
Judy ga piccharishita pantsu wo haiteru toki wa, ore no mesen wa kanojo no asoko no kuikomi ni kugizuke ni natta.

BAD
Most guys are drawn to a woman's breasts, but I am drawn to her camel toe.
たいていの男は女の胸を惹かれるが、オレはアソコの食い込みに惹かれる。
Taitei no otoko wa on'na no mune wo hikareru ga, ore wa asoko no kuikomi ni hikareru.

CHAPTER 10

BIN DONG
ビン・ドン

CHAPTER 10 Bin's Life Story
CD トラック **37**

Bin's Life Story
ビン・ドンの人生

コージの友人だったビンもマフィアの幹部になりました。
今やすっかり悪の道に突き進むビンの人生を見てみましょう。

Bin's Life Story

Bin's family has always had **strong ties** to the Hong Kong Triads, so naturally he joined the family business. Currently, they are enjoying a **flourishing** partnership with the local Yakuza, using cafe shops at fronts for importing **crystal meth** from the mainland. This affords Bin a lot of **cheddar** to spend in establishments such as Club Wakaba. However, Bin is not one to shy away from having to get his hands dirty from time to time.

ビンの家系は代々香港の三合会と強固な繋がりを持っており、彼は自然な成り行きで家族の仕事に携わるようになった。現在は地元のヤクザと手を組んでカフェを隠れ蓑にクリスタル・メスを大陸から輸入しており、クラブ若葉を作れるほどに景気がよく、大金を作った。それでもビンはちょっとした事件でも自分の手を汚すことをためらわない人間であった。

Bin no kakei wa daidai Honkon no sangoukai to kyōkona tsunagari wo motte ori, kare wa shizen'na nariyuki de kazoku no shigoto ni tazusawaru yō ni natta. Genzai wa jimoto no yakuza to te wo kunde kafe wo kakuremino ni kurisutaru mesu wo tairiku kara yunyū shite ori, kurabu wakaba wo tsukureru hodo ni keiki ga yoku taikin wo tsukutta. Soredemo Bin wa chottoshita jiken demo jibun no te wo yogosu koto wo tamerawanai ningendeatta.

If you get in my way, I'll kill you. If you look at me wrong, I'll kill you. If your fart smells, I'll kill you. What did you learn? If there is a scary man in the room, stay in the corner, look away and hold it in.

もしオレの邪魔をしたらお前を殺す。オレのことを見間違えても殺す。もしお前のオナラが臭くても殺す。なにを学んだ？ もし怖い奴が部屋にいたらスミにいろ、そして目をそらしてじっとしてろ。

Moshi ore no jama wo shitara omae wo korosu. Ore no koto wo mi machigaete mo korosu. Moshi omae no onara ga kusakute mo korosu. Nani wo mananda? Moshi kowai yatsu ga heya ni itara sumi ni iro, soshite me wo sorashite jitto shitero.

CHAPTER **10** Words from the story used in phrases

Words from the story used in phrases

物語の単語を使って文を作る

ビンの人生ストーリーのキーワードを使って例文を作ってみましょう。

Words from the Story ストーリーのキーワード

Strong Ties
強固な繋がり

Flourishing
景気のいい

Crystal Meth
クリスタル・メス

Cheddar
大金

Key Word_01

Strong Ties 強固な繋がり

Kyouko na tsunagari

**The strong ties between men,
can never be broken by hoes.**

男同士の強固な繋がりは女によって壊されることは決してない。
Otoko doshi no kyouko na tsunagari wa onna ni yotte kowasareru koto wa keshite nai.

Key Word_02

Flourishing 景気のいい
Keiki no ii

The drug trade is flourishing, due to corrupt officials.

汚職公務員のおかげで薬物売買の景気がよい。

Oshoku koumuin no okagede yakubutsu baibai no keiki ga yoi.

Key Word_03

Crystal Meth クリスタル・メス
Kurisutaru mesu

**Crystal meth is dangerous.
But so is tobacco, so let's smoke!**

クリスタル・メスは危ないけどタバコも同じだ、さあ吸おう！

Kurisutaru mesu wa abunai kedo tabako mo onajida, sa suou!

Key Word_04

Cheddar 大金
Taikin

**As long as you keep the cheddar flowing,
I can supply you with drugs, guns and sex!**

大金を流す限り薬物や拳銃、娼婦を提供できるよ。

Taikin wo nagasu kagiri yakubutsu ya genjuu, shoufu wo teikyou dekiru yo.

CHAPTER 10 Bin's Life Scenario 10

CD トラック 38

1: You cheater!

ズルするなよ!
Zurusurunayo!

3: Are you calling me a liar?

オレのこと嘘つき呼ばわりすんのか!
Ore no koto usotsuki yobawari sun no ka!

**5: Watch what you say!
You might be gambling with more than some chips,
you could be gambling with your life.**

口には気をつけろよ! 今まではチップで賭けてただろうけど、今度はお前の人生を賭けることになるぞ!!
Kuchi ni wa kiotsukero yo! Ima made wa chippu de kaketeta darou kedo, kondo wa omae no jinsei wo kakeru koto ni naru zo!

Bin's Life Scenario 10
ビンの人生シナリオ10「雀荘にて」

ギャンブルをするマイクは大ピンチに陥る。

2: Bullshit! You're cheating!

ざっけんな! お前がズルしてんだろう!
zakken na! Omae ga zurushiten darou!

4: That's right! You're nothing but a two-bit criminal!

当たり前だろ! お前はただの
チンピラだからなっ!
Atarimaedarou! Omae wa tada no chinpira dakarana!

Important Phrases 重要なフレーズ

※Two-bit criminal トゥービット クリミナル
小さな犯罪を犯す犯罪者のこと。
A low-level crook that commits petty crimes.

※Chips チップ
ギャンブルをするためのコインのこと。
Often used form of currency when gambling that can be exchanged for cash.

CHAPTER 10 Things to say to a Triad member...
CD トラック 39

Bin -Things to say to a Triad member...

マフィア（犯罪組織）のビンに使うと怒らせるかも知れないフレーズ10

使うのに注意= ☠ 注意= ☠☠ かなり危険= ☠☠☠

Phrase_01 ☠

Nice tattoos! Can I get one?

格好いい刺青だね、オレにも彫ってくれる？

Kakkou ii irezumi da ne, ore nimo hotte kureru.

Phrase_02
※
Your tattoo is shit, it looks like a kid drew on your back with crayons.

その刺青ダサいですね。子供が背中をクレヨンで描いたみたいですね。

Sono irezumi dasai desu ne. Kodomo ga senaka wo kureyon de egaita mitaidesu ne.

Phrase_03

You look so inconspicuous in your black suit on a hot summer day.

（目立たないように）夏の暑い日でも黒スーツを着ていますね。

(Medatanai you ni) natsu no atsui hi demo kurosutsu wo kitemasu ne.

Phrase_04

Don't hurt me, I'm just passing by.

殴らないで、ただ通るだけですから。

Naguranai de, tada toru dake desu kara.

Phrase_05 ☠☠☠
※
I'd ask you to pinky swear but...

指切りげんまん…あっ…。

Yubikiri genman…a….

Phrase_06
Want a sun visor to go with those tinted windows and sunglasses?
スモークガラスにサングラス、ついでにサンバイザーもどうですか?

Sumōkugarasu ni sangurasu, tsuide ni sanbaizā mo dōdesu ka?

Phrase_07
I thought something something-gumi was a kind of gummy bear.
なんとか、なんとか組は食べるグミだと思ってたんだけど。

nantoka nantoka gumi wa taberu gumi da to omottetanda kedo.

Phrase_08 ☠☠
You must have trouble getting into onsens.
刺青していると温泉に行けませんね。

Irezumi shiteiru to onsen ni ikemasen ne.

Phrase_09
A loan with no contract and no collateral, that is not suspicious at all.
ローンを組むのに契約書もなく保証も必要ないなんて、怪しくないとは言えないですよね。

Rōn wo kumu no ni keiyakusho mo naku hoshō mo hitsuyō nai nante, ayashikunai to wa ienai desu yone.

Phrase_10
I'm not afraid of you, I'm Batman.
あなたなんて怖くないぞ、だってオレはバットマンだもん。

Anata nante kowakunai zo, date ore wa batman damon.

※Phrase_02: せっかく背中の刺青を見せてもらった人に言うのは失礼。

※Phrase_03: inconspicuousは目立たないという意味があり、犯罪組織の人に見えるという表現。

※Phrase_05: アメリカでは「指切りげんまん、うそついたら針千本のます」を "Pinky swear, hope to die, a thousand needles in your eye." とほぼ一緒の意味で使われます。

※Phrase_10: Batman以外にほかのスーパーヒーローを言ったとしてもオタクか変人に思われる率が高いフレーズ。

Bin -Things to say as a Triad member...
マフィア（犯罪組織）のビンが使うフレーズ10

使うのに注意＝ ☠　　注意＝ ☠☠　　かなり危険＝ ☠☠☠

Phrase_01 ☠☠
I'll fucking kill you!
テメーぶっ殺すぞ！
Teme wo bukkorosu zo!

Phrase_02
I'm gonna make you an offer you can't refuse.
お前がが断わることのできないオファーをする。
Kare ga kotowaru koto no dekinai ofa wo suru.

Phrase_03
I aint no rat.
オレはサツ（警察）の犬じゃねぇ。
Ore wa satsu no inu jyane.

Phrase_04
※
It's about honor...and money, lots of money.
名誉と金のためだ…そして金、たくさんの金だ。
Meiyo to kane no tame da… soshite kane takusan no kane da.

Phrase_05 ☠☠☠
Hold out your pinky and we'll see how loyal you really are.
指を詰めてお前の忠誠心を見せてみろや！
Yubi wo tsumete omae no chuseishin wo misete miroya!

Phrase_06 ☠

I don't need a gun to kick your ass, just a reason.

テメーを殺すのに銃は必要ねぇ、ただ仁義があればいい。

Teme wo korosu no ni jyuu wa hitsuyou ne, tada jingi ga areba ii.

Phrase_07
※
Nice place you got here, it'd be a shame if something happened to it.

いい部屋だな、壊すのにはホント惜しいぐらいだ。

Ī heya dana, kowasu no ni wa honto oshī gurai da.

Phrase_08

The best way to enter our business is to be born into※ it.

マフィアはな、生まれつきマフィアなんだよ。

Mafia wa na, umare tsuki mafia nan dayo.

Phrase_09

Extreme problems often require extreme solutions

難しい問題は暴力による解決が必要なときもある。

Muzukashī mondai wa bōryoku ni yoru kaiketsu ga hitsuyōna toki mo aru.

Phrase_10

The last thing I want to do is hurt you. But, it's still on the list.※

本当はお前を痛めつけたくないんだよ、でも仕事だから。

Hontou wa omae wo itame tsuketakunain dayo, demo shigoto dakara.

※Phrase_04: It's about honorは、武士道にみたいに名誉が大事という渋いフレーズ。でもお金も大切って、結局どっちもってこと!?

※Phrase_07: 相手を脅してお金を奪う時に使うフレーズ。お金を出さないと部屋を壊すぞを遠回しに伝えている。

※Phrase_08: なにかの組織やファミリーなどに生まれることを言う。ほか、王室に生まれるなど。

※Phrase_10: 頭にあるリストのこと。

CHAPTER 8 Helpful Words And Phrases GOOD & BAD

シナリオに関連する単語を使ったGOODとBADフレーズ
Helpful Words And Phrases
GOOD & BAD

Cheater 詐欺師 Sagishi

GOOD
Why try hard when you can be a cheater.
詐欺師になるんなら、もっと頑張れ。
Sagishi ni narun nara, motto ganbare.

BAD
I have been called many things like, slut, whore, bitch, and tramp, but never have I been called a cheater!
あたしは尻軽、売女、くそ女、あばずれとかいろんな言われ方をされたけど、詐欺師だけはないわ。
Atashi wa shirigaru, baita, kuso onna, abazure, toka irona iware kata wo sareta kedo, sagishi dake wa nai wa.

luck 運 Un

GOOD
Winning the lottery is nothing but luck, getting laid takes skill!
宝くじに当たるのは運以外のなにものでもないが、セックスはスキルだ!
Takarakuji ni ataru no wa unigai no nani mono demoniaga, sekkusu wa sukiru da!

BAD
Luck has nothing to do with dating a supermodel, it's all about how rich you are.
スーパーモデルとデートするのに運は関係ない、ただどのくらい金持ちかってことだけだ。
Supamoderu to deto suru no ni un wa kankeinai, tada, donogurai kanemochi ka tte koto dake da.

Gambling ギャンブル Gyanburu

GOOD
You shouldn't be gambling your life savings away!
今まで貯めてきたお金をギャンブルで使わない方がいいよ。
Ima made tametekita okane wo gyanburu de tsukawanai hou ga ii yo.

BAD
I took up gambling because my wife is a annoying bitch, and the less I am home the better.
オレはまたギャンブルを始めた、というのも嫁がうるさい女で家にいるよりマシだからだ。
Ore wa mata gyanburu wo hajimeta, toiunomo yome ga urusai onna de, ie ni iru yori mashi dakara da.

Illegal 違法 Ihou

GOOD
You can't play games for money in Japan, it's illegal.
日本ではお金を賭けて遊ぶことはできない、それは違法だ。
Nihon de wa okane wo kakete asobu koto wa dekinai, sore ha ihou da.

BAD
Many things I take comfort in are illegal in Japan. I guess I have to find another country to smoke weed.
オレにとって慰めになる多くのことは日本で違法だ。やっぱりクサを吸うためには別の国を見つけなきゃ。
Ore ni totte nagusame ni naru ooku no koto wa, nihon de ihou da. yappari kusa wo suu tame ni wa betsu no kuni wo mitsukenakya na.

INDEX 牽引

気になった単語があったら、逆引きで検索してみましょう。

A

addiction 中毒	036、039
affair 不倫	086、089
all in one place 賢く	045
all you can drink 飲み放題	058
anal sex アナルセックス	070
asshole クソ野郎	104
attractive 魅力的	057

B

badass ダッセー	116
banana in your pocket もっこりしている	142
beard ヒゲ	105
beautiful 美しい	058
big break 大ブレーク	036、038
bitchin' 文句	107
blackmailing 脅す	048、051
blowjob フェラチオ	068、070
blue tarp home ブルーシートの家	045
body slam 叩き潰す技	026、126
boner 勃起	056
boob grabs オッパイ触る	054
booty sex アナルセックス	142
Booze 酒	012、040
borderline enough ギリギリのところ	106
bring another おかわり	058
bucket バケツ	080
buddies 友だち	110、113
bullshit ざっけんな	151

C

camel toe アソコの食い込み	144
chakras 気	139
cheated 浮気	060、062
cheater 詐欺師	150、156
cheddar 大金	146、149
cherry blossom 桜	046
child labor 未成年労働	084
chins 二重アゴ	129
chips チップ	030、150
chopsticks お箸	118
collateral 保証、担保	153
come out カミングアウト	098、100
complete make-over 化粧直し	081
concerned fan 関心あるファン	092
condom コンドーム	070
crystal meth クリスタル・メス	146、149

D

depression うつ病	048、050
dominate 支配する	123
double お酒のダブル	014、053
dramatic 劇的な	098、101
dumb bitch クソビッチ	078
dump ごたごた	074、077

E

evolution 進化	116

F

fallout 縁が切れる	060、063
feminine フェミニンな	134、136
feminist フェミニスト	108
fired 首になる	036、039
fist こぶし	113
fit 元気	144
flourishing 繁盛／景気のよい	146、149
flying clothesline リングコーナーからジャンプして相手を潰す技	026、127
fuck authority くたばれ政府の犬	111
fuck off どっか行け	013、041
fuck 性交	068
fucking kill you ぶっ殺す	154
fucking squash you ぶっ潰してやる	130
fucking~ 超〜、マジ〜	119

157

INDEX

G

gambling ギャンブル	030、150、156
gangbangs 乱交パーティ	074、077、141
gender 性別	123
getting into 入る	128
ghetto スラム街	120
gonorrhea 淋病	067

H

habit 遊び（癖）	060、063
handjob 手こき、マスタベーション	068
hand shakes 握手	094
hang out 遊んでる	135
hell no 絶対イヤ	102
herpes ヘルペス	067
hit on me 会う	143
hogging ほじくる	080
hold it in じっとする	147
honor 名誉	154

I

I'd ask you to pinky swear 指切りげんまん	152
illegal 違法	156
impotent 勃起不全	014、053
inconspicuous 目立たない	152
involve mud 泥んこプロレス	128

J

jimmy/rubber/condom ゴム	066

K

kinky 変態なこと	066
kiss my ass ふざけるな	142

L

ladyboys オカマ（ニューハーフ）	140
lesbian レズビアン	098、101
lid フタ	080
light touches 太陽が届くところ	043
little shit 小僧	024、114
luck 運	156

M

man crush 想っている男／好きな男性	134、137
masculinity 男らしさ	134、137
mental hospital 精神病院	048、051
milfs 熟女	055
mini skirt ミニスカート	096
minute rice インスタントライス	117

N

nerd オタク	096
nipples 乳首	130
nuts 金玉	141

O

obsession 夢中	086、088
odds 確率	135
oil change オイル交換	108
on the house 店のおごり	015、053
one-night stand ひと晩の相手	135
oral sex 口で行う性行為	022、103
outfit 服	117
ovaries 卵巣	016、065
overpriced 高すぎる値段	081、084

P

parasite lifestyle すねかじり生活	086、089
passion 情熱	122、124
permanent wedgie パンツをお尻に食い込ませる	140
pervert 変態	096
petty theft ちょっとした盗み	110、113
Picnic ピクニック	046
pigs おまわり	120
pimp ポン引き	068
piss オシッコ	094
popular 恰好、人気	122、124
power tools 動力工具	108
pregnant 妊娠	131
prepubescent 思春期前	131
promptly さっさと	086、089
prostitution 売春（をする）	060、063

punk 不良 .... 024、114
put a boot up your ass 殺すほどのこと ... 143
put it on my tab つける 056

R

raise baby 子育て 106
rebel 裏切り者、反抗 120
reborn 生まれ変わった .... 134、137
rechargeable バイブ（大人のおもちゃ） ... 055
repulsive 気持ち悪い 094
respect 敬意 067
retire 引退 .... 122、125
reverse 逆 116
risque 際どい .... 074、076
rock-hard abs 固い腹筋 131

S

sack of shit クソ野郎 044
scandalous 過ち .... 074、077
screwed しくじった 120
sexual harassment セクハラ ..... 036、039
shaved nose to toes 全身脱毛 143
shoot blanks 種無し .... 015、053
shut the fuck up 黙れ 106
skank ブス .... 018、078
sober しらふ 043
soy milk 豆乳 084
spare some change お金くれませんか ... 012、040
sperm 精子 104
spread'em（体の一部を）広げる ..... 028、139
spring 春 046
stab 裏切る 113
stalker ストーカー 096
start the day 一日の始まり 082
stick it in 挿入する 065
still on the list 仕事 155
strap-on ペニスバンド 103
street cred 街の評判 .... 110、113
strong ties 強固な繋がり .... 146、148
stubble 青ひげ 141
stuck 行き詰まる 140

sugar 砂糖 084
sugary 甘ったるい 081
suicide 自殺 .... 048、051
sweaty 汗をかく 144
swing both ways 両天秤にかける 140
syphilis 梅毒 067

T

talk to the hand もういいわ、黙りなさい ... 019、079
teeth point all different directions
ガタガタな歯並び 092
the giant hippy マジヒッピーな人 080
the pill ピル 070
thick 太い 132
thimble 指ぬき 083
tit/titties オッパイ .... 056、132
to be born into 生まれつき 155
too rich for me 自分には高価 ... 021、091
tough as nails 厳しさ .... 098、101
traditional 伝統 132
train fare 電車代 082
transvestites（女装した）オカマ 140
trash ゴミ 046
tune up チューンナップ 108
two-bit criminal 小さい犯罪をおかす者 ... 031、151

U

upskirt パンチラ写真 .... 020、090

W

wedgie パンツの食い込み 144
westerners 西洋人 .... 110、112
wet nap ウェットティッシュ 069
whiskey ウィスキー 058
winnings ファイトマネー、戦利品 ..... 122、125
wipe ふく 105
worship 崇拝 095
wrap up 早く終わらせる 068
wrestle 格闘 132

〈著者〉

ブライアン・レイス
Brian Reyes

ニューヨーク生まれ育ち。高校卒業旅行で日本に魅せられて以来15年間日本在住。公立中・高等学校の英語教師を経て、現在は日本の会社でマーケティング担当者として勤務する。本書は、教師時代に中学校で使っていた教科書をベースになにかできないかと考えたのが原案となった。

DARK HORIZON
おとなになったら使うかも知れない基礎英語

2014年10月20日　初版第1刷
2014年12月22日　初版第2刷

著者・イラスト:ブライアン・レイス
日英文・ネイティブチェック:中島絢
教材CDナレーション:Jimi、Brian、Paul、Anastasia
教材CDプログラム:酒井 宏之(アイズクルー)
装丁・デザイン:CIRCLEGRAPH

発行者　佐野 裕
発行所　トランスワールドジャパン株式会社

〒150-0001　東京都渋谷区神宮前6-34-15 モンターナビル
Tel. 03-5778-8599 / Fax. 03-5778-8743
印刷・製本 中央精版印刷株式会社
ISBN 978-4-86256-147-3
Printed in Japan
©Brian Reyes, Transworld Japan Inc. 2014

◎定価はカバーに表示されています。
◎本書の全部または一部を、著作権法で認められた範囲を超えて
無断で複写、複製、転載、あるいはデジタル化を禁じます。
◎乱丁・落丁本は小社送料負担にてお取り替え致します。